用英语讲中国好故事

寓言故事

（汉英对照）

THE FABLE STORIES

韩 进 ◎ 编著
丁立福 ◎ 译

北京师范大学出版集团
安徽大学出版社

图书在版编目(CIP)数据

寓言故事:汉英对照/韩进编著;丁立福译. —合肥:安徽大学出版社,2021.4
(用英语讲中国好故事)
ISBN 978-7-5664-2211-8

Ⅰ.①寓… Ⅱ.①韩… ②丁… Ⅲ.①寓言—作品集—中国—汉、英 Ⅳ.①I277.4

中国版本图书馆CIP数据核字(2021)第045440号

寓言故事:汉英对照
YUYAN GUSHI: HANYING DUIZHAO

韩 进 编著
丁立福 译

出版发行:北京师范大学出版集团
　　　　　安 徽 大 学 出 版 社
　　　　　(安徽省合肥市肥西路3号 邮编230039)
　　　　　www.bnupg.com.cn
　　　　　www.ahupress.com.cn
印　　刷:安徽省人民印刷有限公司
经　　销:全国新华书店
开　　本:170 mm×240 mm
印　　张:12.75
字　　数:198千字
版　　次:2021年4月第1版
印　　次:2021年4月第1次印刷
定　　价:37.00元
ISBN 978-7-5664-2211-8

策划编辑:李 梅　韦 玮　葛灵知　　　　　装帧设计:丁 健
责任编辑:葛灵知　高婷婷　李 雪　　　　　美术编辑:李 军
责任校对:韦 玮　　　　　　　　　　　　　责任印制:赵明炎

版权所有　侵权必究
反盗版、侵权举报电话:0551—65106311
外埠邮购电话:0551—65107716
本书如有印装质量问题,请与印制管理部联系调换。
印制管理部电话:0551—65106311

前　言

青少年是在故事中成长的，听故事、读故事、讲故事，是他们的最爱。自古流传下来的故事浩如烟海，给他们挑选故事一定要慎之又慎，必须有益于身心健康，能够帮助他们扣好人生精神成长的第一粒扣子。

中华文化源远流长，在先贤留下的无数文化瑰宝中，神话、寓言、成语、童话和民间故事成为青少年必备的精神食粮，哺育他们成长，在薪火相传中延续中华文化的命脉。

每个民族都有自己的神话、寓言、成语、童话和民间故事，共同构成人类文化的宝库。中国的神话、寓言、成语、童话和民间故事蕴含着的中华文化，历来是世界了解中国的一扇窗户、一面镜子和一条捷径。

为弘扬中华文化，让更多海内外青少年更好地了解中华文化，我们编写了这套"用英语讲中国好故事"丛书。本丛书参照教育部统编语文教材推荐阅读书目的范围和要求，选取经过时间检验的神话、寓言、成语、童话和民间故事等经典篇目进行改编创作，在原汁原味讲述故事的同时，力求情节完整，语言流畅，读起来饶有趣味，又开卷有益。

在编排体例上，兼顾中外读者查询方便，以汉语拼音为序排列目录，中英文对照阅读，以清新活泼的风格，亲近读者，满足其阅读期待。具体篇目一般从出处、故事、释义三部分进行解析，做到知识性、趣味性、教

育性、可读性并重。在篇目选择和改编过程中,作者参阅了有关资料,注意汲取同类选本的编写经验,再根据本丛书读者的定位,进行有针对性的阅读辅导。故事虽然还是那些故事,但与现实的联系更加紧密了。

本丛书致力于让青少年读中华文化故事,推动中华文化"走出去",构建人类精神家园。本丛书难免有不足之处,欢迎读者批评指正,以期再版重印时加以修订完善。

韩 进

安徽省文艺评论家协会主席

2021 年 4 月 20 日

目 录
Contents

八哥学舌 1
Mynah Imitating Human Tongue 2
抱薪救火 3
Carrying Faggots to Put out a Fire 4
不禽不兽 6
Neither Birds nor Beasts 7
不死之药 9
Medicine to Make People Immortal 10
不听忠告 12
Failure to Adopt Advice 13
蚕与蛛 15
A Silkworm and a Spider 16
常羊学射 18
Chang Yang Learning Archery 19
楚人习操舟 21
A Man of Chu Steering the Boat 22
楚人学齐语 24
A Boy of Chu Learning the Qi Language 25
唇亡齿寒 27
If the Lips Are Gone, the Teeth Will Be Cold 28

次非杀蛟	30
Ci Fei Killing Flood Dragons	31
大脖子病人	33
Big-neck Patients	34
戴高帽子	36
Presented with "Tall Hats"	37
东郭先生和狼	39
Mr. Dongguo and Wolf	41
给猫取名儿	43
Naming Cat for Bubble Reputation	44
公输刻凤	46
Lu Ban Carving Phoenix	47
海龟和群蚁	49
A Sea Turtle and a Group of Ants	50
海鸟之死	52
Death of the Seabird	53
河豚发怒	54
Globefish Getting Very Angry	55
涸辙之鱼	56
Fish Stranded in Dry Rut	57
后羿射箭	59
Hou Yi Shooting Arrows	60
糊涂的麋鹿	62
A Muddled Elk	63
画鬼最易	65
Easiest to Draw Ghosts	66

纪昌学射	67
Ji Chang Learning Archery	68
击邻家之子	70
Beating up Neighbor's Son	71
棘刺尖儿上雕猴子	73
Monkey Carved on the Thorn Tip	74
姜从树生	76
Ginger Growing on Trees	77
匠石运斤	78
Stonemason Wielding Axe	79
狡生梦金	81
Sly Student Dreaming about Gold	82
截竿进城	84
Entering the City Gate with a Long Pole	85
荆人夜涉	86
Chu Troop Wading Across River at Night	87
客套误事	88
False Etiquette Spoiling Affairs	89
孔雀爱尾	91
Peacocks Cherishing Their Tails	92
良狗捕鼠	94
Good Dog Catching Rats	95
两小儿辩日	96
Two Kids Arguing about the Sun	97
买椟还珠	99
Buying the Casket Without the Pearl	100

卖弄小聪明的猎人	102
Hunter Playing Petty Tricks	103
猫头鹰搬家	105
An Owl Moving Its Nest	106
明年再改	107
Stop Stealing Next Year	108
其父善游	109
The Son of a Good Swimmer	110
齐人偷金	111
A Man of Qi Stealing Gold	112
千金买马首	113
Buying Head of Horse with Gold	114
穷和尚和富和尚	116
Two Monks	117
人贵有自知之明	119
The Significance of Self-knowledge	120
桑中生李	122
Plum Growing out of Mulberry	123
山鸡与凤凰	125
Pheasant and Phoenix	126
生木造屋	128
Mansion Made of Raw Wood	129
宋人疑盗	131
A Man of Song Suspicious of Stealing	132
束氏蓄猫	133
Shu Raising Cats	134

寓言故事

太阳的样子	136
Appearance of the Sun	137
螳螂捕蝉，黄雀在后	139
The Cicada, the Praying Mantis and the Sparrow	140
五十步笑百步	142
The Pot Calling the Kettle Black	143
喜鹊搬家	145
The Magpie's Nest	146
心不在马	147
No Attention to Horses	148
兄弟争雁	150
Brothers Arguing over Wild Geese	151
宣王好射	153
King Xuan Loving Archery	154
薛谭学讴	156
Xue Tan Learning to Sing	157
掩耳盗铃	159
Covering One's Ears to Steal a Bell	160
燕人还国	162
A Man of Yan Returning to His Hometown	164
叶公好龙	167
Lord Ye's Love for Dragons	168
疑邻偷斧	169
Suspecting the Neighbor of Stealing an Axe	170
永某氏之鼠	172
Nobody's Rats in Yongzhou	173

鹬蚌相争	175
A Snipe and a Clam Locked in Fight	176
凿井得人	178
The Man Who Was Found in Well	179
曾子杀猪	180
Why Zengzi Killed the Pig	181
折箭训子	183
Breaking Arrows to Admonish Sons	184
郑人逃暑	185
A Man of Zheng Escaping Summer Heat	186
郑人惜鱼	187
A Man of Zheng Who Cherished Fish	188
捉蝉的学问	190
Know How to Catch Cicadas	191

寓言故事

八哥学舌

《叔苴子》

有一只八哥,经过主人的训练,学会了模仿人说话。它每天颠来倒去就会说那么几句话,却自以为了不起,把谁都不放在眼里。

一天,一只蝉在院子里不停地叫着,八哥听到蝉的叫声后,便对它说:"喂,歇会儿行不行?就会发出单调难听的叫声,叫起来还没完没了,我会学人说话,也不像你那么炫耀。"

蝉微微一笑,说:"你能模仿人说话,确实很好,但你说的不是自己的话,等于没说。我虽然叫得单调一些,可表达的是我自己的意思啊!"

八哥听了,满脸通红,羞愧地低下了头。从此以后,八哥再也不跟主人学舌了。

【寓意】不要一味地去模仿别人,否则会失去自己。

Mynah Imitating Human Tongue

From *Shu Ju Zi*

There was a **mynah** who learned to imitate a few human words after having been trained by his master. He could only repeat the same words every day, but he thought he was great and **looked down upon** anyone else.

One day, when the mynah heard a **cicada** was screaming endlessly in the yard, he said to his playmate, "Hey, can't you take a break? You're making **monotonous**, unpleasant noises and crying without stop. I can speak like human beings, but I don't show off as you do."

The cicada smiled and said, "It is very good indeed that you can imitate human speech; but what you said is not from your own brain, which is the same as not saying them. However, what I cried for may be a bit more monotonous, but it's my own words!"

When the mynah heard, he **flushed** all his face and bowed in shame. From then on, he would never imitate human tongue from his owner again.

❋ **Moral**

Don't try to imitate others blindly, or we will lose ourselves.

---

mynah
n. 八哥

look down upon
瞧不起，看不上

cicada
n. 蝉

monotonous
adj. 单调乏味的

flush
v. 发红，脸红

抱薪救火

《史记》

战国时期,秦国最为强大,魏国毗邻秦国,屡次遭受秦国的侵略,损兵失地。当秦国又一次攻打魏国时,多数大臣都劝说魏王,以黄河以北和太行山以南的大片土地为代价,向秦王求和。

谋士苏代不以为然,他一贯主张"合纵抗秦",各诸侯国联合起来抵抗秦国。苏代得知魏王欲割地求和的事后,就对魏王说:"侵略者都是贪得无厌的,你想用领土、权利去换取和平,是办不到的。只要你的国土还在,就无法满足侵略者的欲望。这好比抱着柴草去救火,情况只会越来越糟;柴草一把一把地投入火中,火怎么能被扑灭呢?柴草一天不烧完,火是一天不会熄灭的。"

尽管苏代讲得头头是道,但是胆小的魏王始终拿不定主意,他只顾眼前的太平,一味地委曲求全,还是把魏国大片的土地割让给秦国。最终,魏国被秦国所灭。

【寓意】用错误的方法去消除灾害,不但不能消除灾害,反而导致灾害更大。对侵略者决不能割地求和,而应该血战到底。

Carrying Faggots to Put out a Fire

From *Historical Records*

During the Warring States Period, Qin State was the most powerful among the seven states. It waged war on Wei State in its neighborhood, making Wei State suffering heavy casualties and loss of territory. When Wei State was attacked for another time, most officials persuaded the King to sue for peace with Qin State by **ceding** the area of the northern Yellow River and the southern Taihang Mountains.

However, the minister and strategist Su Dai not only opposed but also advocated the idea of "making the vertical and horizontal **alliance** to resist Qin". He said to the King of Wei, "Your Majesty, all invaders are greedy and **insatiable**, so you can't successfully sue for peace with your land and rights, and they will never be satisfied so long as your territory remains. Ceding for peace won't work. It's just like carrying **faggots** to put out a fire, only to make the situation even worse. Thus, how can the fire be extinguished when bunches of firewood are added into flames one by one? The fire will not be extinguished until the firewood is burned out one day."

Unfortunately, the King of Wei failed to make up his mind in spite of Su Dai's **eloquent** speech. The cowardly

cede
v. 割让，转让

alliance
n. 同盟，联盟

insatiable
adj. 贪得无厌的

faggot
n. 柴捆

eloquent
adj. 雄辩的，流利的

King was only concerned about the peace for the time being and still ceded the large territory to Qin State, and his state was extinguished by Qin State in the end.

Moral

If we use the wrong method to eliminate the disaster, we will not only not eliminate it but will result in even greater damage. In the face of the invaders we should never cede territory for peace but fight to the end.

不禽不兽

《笑府》

百鸟之王凤凰要过生日了，所有的鸟都前来祝寿，只有蝙蝠没来，凤凰担心蝙蝠出了什么事情。

一天，凤凰看见在树上睡懒觉的蝙蝠，就问道："蝙蝠老弟，你处在我管辖的森林里，我生日那天怎么没见你来呀？"

蝙蝠说："我有脚，属于兽类，不归你管，为什么要去给你贺寿呢？"凤凰想想也有道理，就不再怪罪蝙蝠。

过了几天，走兽之王麒麟过生日，蝙蝠也没有去。麒麟也为蝙蝠担心。

后来，麒麟遇到正在树上懒洋洋睡觉的蝙蝠，问道："最近可好啊，蝙蝠老弟？我生日那天怎么没有见到你呀？"

蝙蝠似醒非醒地说："我有翅膀，属于飞禽，不归你管，我为什么要向你祝寿呢？"麒麟想想也有道理，此事就这么算了。

后来麒麟和凤凰见了面，它们说到蝙蝠的事，才知道了真相，相互感叹地说："现在世上风气恶劣，偏偏生出这样一些不禽不兽的家伙，真拿它们没办法！"

【寓意】比喻一些卑鄙无耻的人没有明确的立场，常常根据自己的需要改换身份。

Neither Birds nor Beasts

From *Xiao Fu*

As the queen of all birds, a **phoenix** was going to have her birthday, and all birds came to celebrate, only except a bat. The phoenix was worried about what's happening to the bat.

One day, the phoenix saw the bat dozing off in a tree, and asked him, "Brother Bat, you are in the forest under my **jurisdiction**. Why didn't you come on my birthday?"

The bat replied, "I have the feet of beasts, and am not in your charge. Why should I go to celebrate your birthday?" The phoenix thought it made sense, so she stopped blaming him.

A few days later, a **kylin**, the king of the beasts, was going to celebrate his birthday, and the bat didn't come either. The kylin was worried about him, too.

One day, the kylin met the bat dozing off in a tree, and asked, "How are you, Brother Bat? Why didn't I see you on my birthday?"

The bat seemed to wake up and said, "Why should I go to celebrate your birthday, for I have the wings of birds and am not in your charge?" The kylin thought it made sense, so the matter was settled.

Later, the kylin and the phoenix met each other. They

phoenix
n. 凤凰

jurisdiction
n. 管辖区域

kylin
n. 麒麟

talked about the bat and found the truth about him, sighing to each other, "Nowadays the world is in a bad condition and some creatures appear belonging to neither birds nor beasts. There is really nothing we can do about them!"

Moral

Metaphorically speaking, some **despicable** and shameless persons do not have a clear position, and often change their identities according to what they need.

despicable
adj. 卑鄙的

不死之药

《战国策》

古时候,传说世上有一种药,人吃了就可以长生不死,许多君王都想得到它,故而有些人借此拿假药来骗钱。

有一天,有人来到楚国都城,说要将长生不死之药献给楚王。楚王听了很欢喜,命令内臣取药。这个内臣捧着药进宫去,在路上碰到宫中的卫士,问他拿的是什么东西。送药的人说:"这是长生不死药。"卫士问:"可以吃吗?"送药的人说:"可以吃。"于是卫士一把抢过药来,自己吃了。

楚王知道后大怒,要杀了这个卫士。卫士托人向楚王解释说:"我问送药的人,他告诉我说是可以吃的,我才拿过药来吃下去。这事我没有罪,有罪的乃是送药的人。况且客人所献的是长生不死药,我吃了药大王就杀我,这岂不成了'丧生药',是客人欺骗大王。大王杀死一个没有罪的人,正好证明有人在欺骗大王,您不如把我放了。"

楚王听了卫士的话觉得有道理,就放了他。而那所谓的长生不死药,当然是假的了。

【寓意】卫士用"不死之药"变"丧生药"作假设,以不让楚王声誉受损为名,阻止了可能引来的杀身之祸,表面看是卫士能言善辩,实质上是世界上从来就没有什么长生不死之药。

Medicine to Make People Immortal

From *Stratagems of the Warring States*

In ancient times, a medicine was said to make people **immortal**, so many kings wanted it and some people even tried to cheat for money with the fake medicine.

One day, someone came to the capital of Chu State, and said he wanted to offer the King of Chu the **longevity** medicine. The King of Chu was very happy to hear and ordered his royal official in court to fetch the medicine. When the official came back into the palace with the medicine, he met the palace guard and was asked what he was sending. The man said, "It is the medicine to make people immortal." The guard asked, "Can I have it?" The man who delivered the medicine replied, "Yes, you can." Thus, the guard **snatched** the medicine and had it himself.

The King of Chu was furious and wanted to kill the guard after he found out. The guard entrusted someone to explain to the King, "I asked the person who delivered the medicine and was told that I could have it, so I took the medicine and had it. I instead of the person is **innocent**. Moreover, what the guest offered is the medicine for immortality. If you want to kill me for I had it, the medicine would be certainly 'fatal medicine', which shows the guest deceived you. You would like to kill an innocent

immortal
adj. 不朽的，不死的

longevity
n. 长寿，长命

snatch
v. 抢走，一把夺去

innocent
adj. 无辜的，清白的

man, just proving that someone is deceiving you. Thus, why don't you let me go?"

The King of Chu heard the guard's words, thinking that the words made sense, and let him go. As for the so-called medicine to make people immortal, it is actually fake.

❖ Moral

In the name of not harming the reputation of the King, based on the hypothesis that "the medicine to make people immortal" turning into the "fatal medicine", the guard prevented himself from being killed, which appeared to be his eloquence but proved in reality the medicine to keep immortal does not exist in the world at all.

不听忠告

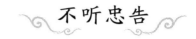

《说苑》

有户人家的烟囱砌得太直,一烧火就直冒火星儿。烟囱旁边还堆着一大堆柴禾。有位客人看见这种情况,就提醒主人:"这样太危险了,会失火的。您把烟囱改造一下,砌个弯道;柴禾也不要放得那么近才好。"主人不答话,根本没有听进去客人的忠告。

没过几天,由于火星儿落进柴堆,果然失火了。幸亏众乡邻来得及时,奋力扑救,才没有造成严重的损失。

第二天,主人杀猪宰羊,大摆宴席,答谢救火的乡邻,按出力大小依次入座。那位最早提出忠告的人,主人压根儿没想到应该请他入席。如果这位主人能听从忠告,既不会发生火灾,也无需浪费酒肉了。

【寓意】防患于未然。失火人家的可悲,不仅在于事先不听忠告,还在于事后依然没有认识到忠告的价值。

寓言故事

Failure to Adopt Advice

From *The Garden of Anecdotes*

One family's chimney was built so straight that sparks would come out directly once the fire was lighted. Besides, there was a big pile of firewood next to the chimney. When a guest saw it, he reminded the house owner, "It's too dangerous, and easy to catch fire. **Remodeling** the chimney with a bend will be a good way; it's better not to put the firewood so close to it." The owner said nothing, and **turned a deaf ear to** the guest's words.

In a few days, as sparks fell into the woodpile, the house did catch fire. Fortunately, all the neighbors came in time and fought to put it out, so no serious damage was brought.

The next day, the owner held a big banquet by serving pork and mutton to thank the neighbors who put out the fire. They were seated in the order of their contribution. However, as for the person who gave advice at first, the owner did not even think that he should be invited to the banquet. If the owner had adopted his advice, there would have been no fire and no need to treat others with **extravagance**.

remodel

v. 改变……的结构

turn a deaf ear to

充耳不闻

extravagance

n. 奢侈

❖ Moral

Prevention is better than cure. The tragedy of the fire-stricken family is not only that its owner didn't listen to the advice beforehand, but also he still didn't realize the value of the advice afterwards.

蚕与蛛

《雪涛小说》

有一天,蜘蛛对蚕说:"你每天吃饱桑叶,一天天长大,然后从嫩黄的嘴里吐出纵横交叉的长丝,织成茧壳,把自己牢牢地封裹起来。蚕妇把你放进开水中,抽出长丝,最后毁了你的身躯和茧壳。你口吐银丝的绝技恰恰成了杀死自己的手段,这样做不是太愚蠢了吗?"

蚕回答:"我固然是杀死了自己,但我吐出的银丝可以织成精美的绸缎,皇帝穿的龙袍、百官穿的朝服,哪一件不是用我吐出的银丝织成的?你也有吐丝织网的绝技。你张开罗网,坐镇中央,蝴蝶、蜜蜂、蚊子、小虫只要撞入你的罗网,就统统成了你口中的美餐,无一幸免。你的技术是够高超的了,但专门用来捕杀别的动物,是不是太残忍了呢?"

蜘蛛很不以为然:"为别人打算,说得多好听!我宁愿为自己!"

唉,世上宁愿像蚕一样而不愿像蜘蛛一样的人太少了。

【寓意】蚕和蜘蛛的对话反映了两种不同的人生观:为别人还是为自己。蚕的牺牲精神和蜘蛛的自私形成鲜明的对比,做人应该像蚕一样。

A Silkworm and a Spider

From *Xuetao Novel*

One day, a spider said to a silkworm, "You feed on mulberry leaves every day, growing up gradually, and then spit the long, crisscrossing threads from your bright yellow mouth. Afterwards, you weave them into a cocoon shell, and seal yourself up tightly. The silkworm-raising woman puts you in boiling water, draws out the silks, and finally destroys your body and cocoon shell. Wouldn't it be foolish to do this when your stunt of spitting silver silks becomes precisely the means to kill yourself?"

The silkworm replied, "It is the truth that I will kill myself sooner or later, but the silver thread I spit out can be woven into fine silk. Take a look at the dragon robe worn by the emperor, or the court dress worn by civil and military officials. Aren't they woven with the silks I spit out? You also have a **knack** for spitting silks and weaving webs. Having finished weaving the web, you just wait in the center, and as long as butterflies, bees, mosquitoes, and small insects run into your web, they all become a delicious meal in your mouth, no one being spared. Your technique is superb enough, but isn't it too cruel to use it specifically to hunt and kill other animals?"

The spider was very unimpressed, "Planning for

knack
n.（天生或学会的）技能，本领

others, how nice to say! I'd rather plan for myself!"

Alas, there are too few people in the world who would rather behave like the silkworm than like the spider.

Moral

The dialogue between the silkworm and the spider reflects two different views of life: for others or for themselves. The **self-sacrifice** of the silkworm and the selfishness of the spider are presenting a sharp contrast and we should behave like the silkworm.

self-sacrifice

n. 自我牺牲，忘我精神

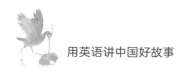

常羊学射

《郁离子》

常羊拜屠龙子朱为师学习射箭。屠龙子朱对常羊讲了一个蕴含射箭道理的小故事:

有一次,楚王在云梦泽打猎。他让手下把豢养的禽兽全部驱赶出来,供自己狩猎。一时间,天空禽鸟齐飞,满地走兽奔逐。几只梅花鹿在楚王的马左边蹦跳,一群麋鹿在楚王的马右边追逐。楚王举弓搭箭,一会儿对准梅花鹿,一会儿对准麋鹿,正想放箭,一只天鹅又扇动两只大翅膀从楚王头上飞过,馋得他又把弓箭指向空中。就这样,楚王瞄了半天,一箭没放,不知道该射哪个好了。这时候,有个叫养叔的大夫对楚王说:"我射箭的时候,把一片树叶放在百步之外,射十次中十次。如果放上十片叶子,那么能不能射中,就很难说了。"

常羊听了这个故事,连连点头,从中受到了很大启发。

【寓意】做任何事情必须专心致志,专注于主要目标。三心二意,左顾右盼,将一事无成。

Chang Yang Learning Archery

From *Yu Li Zi*

Chang Yang came to learn archery under the guidance of Tu Longzizhu, who told a story that contained principles of archery in it.

Once, the King of Chu State was hunting around Yunmeng Lakes. He asked his men to drive out all the animals in **captivity** for his own hunting. For a while, birds in the sky flew together and animals ran all over the ground. A few sika deer jumped on the left of the King's horse, and a herd of elk ran on the right. The King of Chu raised his bow and arrow, one moment to a sika deer and the other to an elk. As he was about to release the arrow, a swan **fluttered** two large wings over the head of the King of Chu, and he greedily pointed the arrow into the air. In this way, the King aimed for a long time, but he didn't release any arrow for not knowing which one to shoot. At this time, an official named Yang Shu said to the King, "When I shoot, I put one leaf as the target a hundred paces away and shoot it ten times without any missing. However, if I put ten leaves, it's hard to say whether I can hit it or not."

After hearing this story, Chang Yang nodded again and again, being inspired a lot.

captivity

n. 关押，围住

flutter

v. 挥动，振（翅）

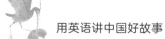

Moral

We must be attentive to everything we do and focus on the main goal. If we are half-hearted, we will accomplish nothing.

寓言故事

楚人习操舟

《贤奕编》

　　楚国有一个人非常认真地跟着老师学习驾船。他按照老师的指导，快划、慢划、转弯、掉头，刻苦练习基本功。

　　基本学习课程结束后，他驾着小船到江中岛屿之间的小河里练习，按照老师教的要领，得心应手。他自以为已经完全学会了驾船的技术，于是立即谢别了老师，要驾船到外面闯荡世界。

　　告别老师后，楚人驾着小船冲出小河，一路风景，让他欣喜不已。突然小船驶入一段激流险滩，水中怪石林立，水流湍急，老师教的技术无法应对突如其来的险情。楚人心中慌张，四处张望，手忙脚乱，船桨掉入江中，小船颠簸摇晃，失去了控制。然而现在的危险，不就是之前侥幸所造成的吗？

【寓意】楚人落水的结果可想而知，而悲剧的根源在于自以为是、骄傲自满。不能略有新知就骄傲自满，略有进步就妄自尊大，否则逃脱不了失败的命运。

A Man of Chu Steering the Boat

From *Xian Yi Bian*

In the Chu State, a man learned to steer a boat from his teacher very carefully. He practiced the rowing basics assiduously, such as **paddling** fast or slowly, turning right or left and making a U-turn, according to his teacher's instruction.

paddle
v. 划船

After accomplishing the basic learning course, he took his boat to a small river between the islands, practiced his skills and performed with ease according to essentials taught by his teacher. He thought he had completely learned the skills of rowing a boat, so he immediately thanked the teacher, and wanted to drive his boat into the outside world.

After saying goodbye to his teacher, the man of Chu drove his boat out of the river, the beautiful scenery along the way making him delighted. Suddenly his boat entered a section of **rapids** and dangerous shoals, with the water being lined with strange rocks and the current wheezing, and the skills taught by his teacher was not unable to deal with such sudden danger. The man of Chu felt panic, looked around and acted with total confusion. The oars dropping into the river, his boat jolted and **swayed** out of control. However, the danger **encountered** then was

rapids
n. 急流，湍急的河水

sway
v. 摇晃，摇摆

caused by the previous luck, wasn't it?

❖ Moral

The outcome can be predicted that the man of Chu fell into the river. The root of such tragedy is self-righteousness and complacency. We cannot **be complacent about** a little new knowledge and arrogant with a little progress, or we will not escape the fate of failure.

encounter
v. 遭遇

be complacent about
自满，自鸣得意

楚人学齐语

《孟子》

一天,孟子对宋国大臣戴不胜说:"如果有个楚国的大夫想让自己的儿子学说齐国语言,您看是请齐国人教他好呢,还是请楚国人教他好呢?"

戴不胜笑着回答说:"当然是请齐国人教他。"

孟子笑了笑,说:"一个齐国人教他固然不错,但他身边的人都是楚国人,说楚国话,哪怕用鞭子来抽打他,逼迫他学齐话,他也不可能学好。如果把他送到齐国都城,那里有最繁华的街市,让他在那里住上几年,那么,就算天天用鞭子抽打他,要他说楚国话,他也做不到了。"

【寓意】环境对人的影响是很大的。学习语言,需要有语言环境。人的品德培养也是一样的,所谓近朱者赤,近墨者黑。

A Boy of Chu Learning the Qi Language

From *Mencius*

One day, Mencius asked Dai Busheng, a minister of Song State, "If a high official of Chu State wants his son to learn the language of Qi State, do you think it would be better to ask a person from Qi State to teach him, or a person from Chu State to teach him?"

Dai Busheng replied with a smile, "Of course, he should be taught by a person from Qi State."

Mencius laughed and said, "It is good to be taught by a teacher from Qi State, but he is in fact surrounded by his fellowmen who speak Chu's tongue. Even if he were **whipped**, it would still be difficult for him to master the Qi language well. If he were sent to the capital of Qi State and allowed to live there for a few years, where there are the most **prosperous** markets, it would be impossible to force him, even with a whip, to speak Chu's tongue again."

whip

v. 鞭打

prosperous

adj. 繁荣的，兴旺的

❖ Moral

The environment has a great influence on people. To learn a language, we need an environment. The same is true for human character development, just as the saying goes, "If you lie down with dogs, you will get up with fleas."

唇亡齿寒

《左传》

春秋时期，晋国的近邻有虢（guó）、虞两个小国。有一年，晋国想攻打虢国，但晋国和虢国之间夹着虞国，要攻打虢国必须经过虞国。晋献公担心虞国不会同意借路，焦虑不安。

这时，晋国的大夫荀息建议，将晋献公的宝玉和骏马作为礼物送给虞王，以求借道。晋献公怕虞王收下礼物也不肯借路，荀息说："他若不答应借路，就不会收下礼物。如果收下，就一定会借路给我们。那些礼物只是暂时属于他们，我们最后还能收回来。把宝玉放在虞国，就像从内室移到外室；把宝马送给虞国，就像把马从圈里牵出来养在圈外，您怕什么呢？"

于是，晋献公依据荀息的计策，把礼物送到虞国，请求借道。虞国国王见到礼物非常高兴，便爽快地答应借道。虞王手下有一个名叫宫之奇的大臣，极力劝阻虞王说："我们不能借路给晋国。虢国是我们的友邻，和我们虞国的关系就好像是嘴唇和牙齿一样，没有了嘴唇，牙齿就会感到寒冷。一旦晋国灭掉虢国，我们虞国也就难保了。借道给晋国万万使不得。"虞王不听。

果然，晋国军队借道虞国，消灭了虢国。回来时，借口整顿兵马，驻扎在虞国，发动突然袭击，又灭掉了虞国。

【寓意】"唇亡齿寒"比喻双方关系密切，相互依存。寓言中的虞王贪图小利，不听劝谏，带来灭国之灾，既害人又害己。

If the Lips Are Gone, the Teeth Will Be Cold

From *Zuo's Commentary on Spring and Autumn Annals*

During the Spring and Autumn Period, Jin State had two small and immediate neighbors, states of Guo and Yu. One year, Jin State wanted to **invade** Guo State but had to pass through the territory of Yu State since it sandwiched between Jin and Guo. The King Xian of Jin was anxious that Yu State would not agree to allow the Jin army to pass.

At that time, Xun Xi, a senior official of Jin, suggested the King Xian of Jin should send the special gifts of precious jade and fine horses to the King of Yu in order to pass. The King Xian of Jin hesitated that the King of Yu would accept the gifts but refuse to give the way. Xun Xi explained, "If he refuses to let us pass, he will not accept our gifts; if he accepts the gifts, he will definitely give us the way. The precious gifts will be his temporarily and will **eventually** return to us. Putting the precious jade in Yu State is like moving it from the inner chamber to the outer chamber; giving the fine horse to Yu State is like taking a horse out of the inner stable to an outer stable. So what are you afraid of?"

Therefore, the King Xian of Jin, following Xun Xi's

invade
v. 侵略，侵犯

eventually
adv. 最终

advice, had the gifts sent to the King of Yu and asked to use the way. The latter was very pleased to see the gifts and immediately granted the request. Gong Zhiqi, one of senior officials beside the King of Yu, objected, "We cannot give the way to Jin. Guo State is our friendly neighbor; it relates to us as lips are to teeth, depending on each other for survival. If the lips are gone, the teeth will get cold. Once Jin State destroys Guo State, Yu State will be in danger. It is absolutely impossible for us to give the way to Jin State." The King of Yu turned a deaf ear to Gong Zhiqi's warning.

Sure enough, the Jin army soon **wiped out** Guo State after passing through Yu State. When **retreating** with success, they stationed themselves in Yu State on the pretext of consolidating their own soldiers and horses, and destroyed Yu State by launching a surprise attack.

wipe out
消灭
retreat
v. 退回

❀ Moral

The idiom refers to the close relationship and interdependence between two sides. In the fable, the King of Yu, greedy for small profits, did not listen to advice, which led to the destruction of his state, not only harming others but also himself.

次非杀蛟

《吕氏春秋》

楚国有位勇士叫次非,他在吴国得到一把锋利的宝剑。在回乡途中,他乘坐一只木船过江。

渡船刚到江中,突然有两条蛟龙左右围住了渡船。船上的乘客个个被吓得魂飞魄散,摇船的人被吓得手脚哆嗦。次非问摇船人:"为什么会这样?"摇船人告诉他,过去有船只被两条蛟龙缠住,船上的人没有能够活命的。

次非"唰"地拔出宝剑,对船上的人说:"大家不要惊慌,我来收拾这两条恶龙。"大家都为他担心,有人劝他不要冒险。次非要给大家鼓气,坚定地说:"它们只不过是江中的一堆腐肉朽骨罢了!如果我舍弃宝剑能保全众人的生命,那我为什么要吝惜这宝剑呢!"说完便纵身跃入江中,跟恶龙搏斗,终于杀了恶龙,保全船上人的生命。

当次非回到船上时,大家叫他救命恩人,称赞他是大英雄。

【寓意】危难关头,需要有人挺身而出,拯救别人,也成全了自己。这种迎难而上的牺牲精神是中华民族的优秀品质。

Ci Fei Killing Flood Dragons

From *Master Lü's Spring and Autumn Annals*

A warrior named Ci Fei from Chu State once got a sharp sword in Wu State. On his way back to his hometown, he crossed a river on a wooden boat.

As soon as the ferry reached the middle of the river, it was suddenly surrounded by two flood dragons. The passengers on board were all scared out of their wits, and the man who was rowing the boat was trembling with fear. Ci Fei asked the boatman, "Why is it happening?" The boatman told him that no one on board had been able to **survive** when the boat had been entangled by two flood dragons before.

With a swish, Ci Fei pulled out his sword and said to the people on the boat, "Don't be afraid. I'll deal with the two evil dragons." Everyone was worried about him, and some advised him not to take any risks. Ci Fei tried to cheer everyone up and announced firmly, "They are just a pile of rotten flesh and bones in the river. If I can save the lives of all by giving up the sword, why should I be stingy with it?" After saying that, he jumped into the river, **fought against** these evil dragons, killed them at last, and saved the lives of all the people on the boat.

When Ci Fei returned to the boat, all the people called

survive

v. 生还，幸存

fight against

搏斗

him their savior and praised him as a great hero.

❖ Moral

At a critical moment, someone needs to step forward to save others and be a hero. The spirit of sacrifice is an excellent quality of the Chinese nation.

寓言故事

大脖子病人

《贤奕编》

南岐(qí)这个地方处在陕西、四川一带的山谷中。那里的居民很少与山外的人交往。那里的水很甜，但是缺碘。常年饮用这种水的人，就会得大脖子病，所以南岐的居民没有一个人脖子不大的。

有一天，从山外来了一个人，没有大脖子，这可引起了轰动。南岐的居民，不分男女老幼，都跑来看稀奇，看这个山外人的笑话，大家七嘴八舌地议论开了："你看那人的脖子，又细又长，和我们的不一样，一定是得了什么病。"有人说："这么细的脖子，太丑了，怎么不用围巾围起来呢？这样还到处跑，就不知道难看吗？"

山外人一点也不生气，对村里人说："你们的脖子臃肿凸起，那是得了大脖子病，应该吃药医治。像我这样的脖子，才是正常健康的。"

大家听了，觉得这个山外人少见多怪，说："我们全村人的脖子从来都是这样的，何必去治它呢！就是你出钱给我们治，我们还不干呢！"

他们始终不知道自己的丑陋。

【寓意】长期的闭关自守会使人孤陋寡闻、夜郎自大，听不见忠告，甚至发展到以丑为美、是非颠倒、黑白混淆的地步。

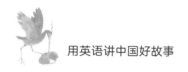

Big-neck Patients

From *Xian Yi Bian*

Nanqi was located in the valleys of Shaanxi and Sichuan regions. The **inhabitants** there rarely interacted with persons outside the mountains. The water there was sweet, but lacking in iodine. Persons who drank the water all year round would get the big-neck disease (endemic goiter). Thus, all of the local residents had a big neck.

One day, from outside the mountains came a man without a big neck, which really caused a sensation. The inhabitants in Nanqi, regardless of men and women, old and young, all came out to **witness** the strangeness. When they amused themselves by watching the stranger outside the mountains, they all **jabbered** in different ways, "Look at that man's neck, so thin and long, unlike ours. He must have some kind of disease." Even someone gabbled, "Such a thin neck is so ugly. Why don't you put a scarf around it? Don't you know it's ugly to be running around like this?"

The outsider was not angry at all, and said to the villagers, "You have the bloated and bulging necks, which are caused by a big-neck disease, and you should take medicine to cure it. A neck like mine is normal and healthy."

After listening everyone thought the outsider got

---

inhabitant

n. 居民

witness

v. 当场看到，见证

jabber

v. 急促兴奋地说

寓言故事

easily surprised because of his ignorance, and said, "The necks of all the persons in our village have always been like this, so why bother to treat it? Even if you pay for our treatment, we still won't do it!"

They still don't know how ugly they are.

* **Moral**

The long-term **seclusion** can lead to isolation, arrogance, and a failure to adopt advice, even to the point of regarding ugliness as beauty, turning right and wrong upside down, and confusing black and white.

seclusion

n. 隐居，与世隔绝

戴高帽子

《一笑》

　　民间俗语把喜欢别人当面奉承自己的行为,叫作喜欢"戴高帽"。

　　有个京官要到外地去任职,离京前去向他的老师告别。他的老师说:"地方官不容易做,当谨慎些。"

　　那人说:"我准备了一百顶高帽,遇到人就送他一顶,应当不至于有意见不合的人。"

　　老师生气地说:"为什么要这样呢?我们要以正直的行为对待所有人。"

　　那人说:"天下像老师您这样不喜欢戴高帽的人,能有几个呢?"

　　老师点了点头,表示赞同地说:"你说的也不无道理。"

　　那人告别老师出来时,对别人说:"我原来有一百顶高帽子,但是现在只剩下九十九顶了。"

【寓意】当局者迷。后人用"戴高帽子"来比喻对别人说恭维的话。

Presented with "Tall Hats"

From *Jokebook*

In a folk saying, people call flatteries to someone's face "presenting a tall hat" to someone, which is called "dai gaomao" in Chinese.

There was a capital official who was going to take up a post in a local area, and before leaving the capital, he went to **bid farewell to** his teacher. His teacher said, "It's not easy to be an official outside the capital, so be careful."

The man said, "I have prepared one hundred 'tall hats', and I will give one to each person I meet; I'm sure all the local people will be pleased."

The teacher said angrily, "Why should we behave like this as long as we treat everyone with **integrity**?"

The man said, "How few people in the world are like you who dislike being flattered or presented with tall hats, dear teacher!"

Hearing this, the teacher was very much pleased. He nodded and said, "Your words make sense."

When the man bade the teacher goodbye and went out, he said to the others, "I used to have a hundred 'tall hats', but now only ninety-nine are left."

bid farewell to
再见

integrity
n. 诚实正直

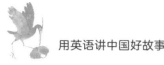

Moral

Those closely involved can not see clearly. "Presented with 'tall hats' " was later used as a metaphor for saying compliments to others.

东郭先生和狼

《东田文集》

春秋时期,晋国大夫赵简子外出打猎,射穿了一只狼的前腿。那狼仓皇逃窜,赵简子穷追不舍。

当时,东郭先生要去中山国谋官,赶着一匹驮着一大袋书简的毛驴,迷路了,正站在路口张望。狼突然窜出来,可怜地对他说:"我被人追赶,求先生救救我,请让我藏进您的书袋里!我躲过了这次劫难,一定报答您的救命之恩。"东郭先生想了想,不能见死不救,就让狼藏到书袋里。

不一会儿,赵简子来到东郭先生跟前,打听有没有看到一只受伤的狼。东郭先生故作镇定地摇着头说:"没看见,没看见。"

赵简子走后,狼在书袋里说:"多谢先生搭救,请放我出来,受我一拜吧!"可是狼一出袋子,立马改口说:"刚才亏你救我,让我大难不死。现在我饿得要命,你救人救到底,就让我吃了吧!"说着就向东郭先生扑去。东郭先生又怕又气,慌忙躲闪,围着毛驴与狼周旋起来。

这时,来了一位拄着拐杖的老人,东郭先生急忙请老人主持公道。老人听了事情的经过,对狼说:"你为什么背叛对你有救命之恩的人呢?"狼为自己辩解道:"您别听他胡说八道,他刚才把我塞进书袋里,用绳子捆绑我的手脚,用书简压住我的身躯,分明是想把我闷死在这不透气的书袋里,这样的人我不该吃掉吗?"

老人想了想,说:"你们各说各有理,我难以裁决。俗话说'眼见为实'。你们把刚才的情形再演示一遍让我看看,我就可以为你们作证。你就可以心安理得地吃他了。"狼高兴地听从了老人的劝说,又让东郭先生捆绑了手脚,重新装进书袋里。这时,老人举起藜杖,狠狠地朝狼打去。

【寓意】人应该善良,但要明辨是非,不应该怜惜像狼一样的恶人。"东郭先生"专指那些不辨是非而滥施同情心的人,"中山狼"则指忘恩负义、恩将仇报的人。

Mr. Dongguo and Wolf

From *Anthology Compiled by Ma Dongtian*

During the Spring and Autumn Period, Zhao Jianzi, a senior official of Jin State, once went out hunting and shot through the foreleg of a wolf. The wolf **fled** in haste, and Zhao Jianzi pursued it relentlessly.

At that time, Mr. Dongguo, who was going to the Zhongshan State to seek an official post, got lost with a donkey carrying a big bag of bamboo books and was standing at the intersection looking around. The wolf suddenly darted out and said to him pitifully, "I'm being chased. Please help me, sir. Let me hide in your book bag. If I could escape this calamity, I will definitely **reciprocate** you for saving my life." Mr. Dongguo thought its request over and decided not to leave it in the lurch, so he let the wolf hide in his book bag.

Soon, Zhao Jianzi came to Mr. Dongguo and inquired if he had seen an injured wolf. Mr. Dongguo shook his head calmly and said, "No, I haven't seen it."

After Zhao Jianzi left, the wolf in the bag said, "Thank you, sir, for rescuing me. Please let me out and accept my **obeisance**." However, as soon as the wolf was out of the bag, it immediately changed its words and said, "Thank you for rescuing me and saving me from death. Since I'm starving to death now, just help me to the end

flee
v. 逃跑

reciprocate
v. 报答

obeisance
n. 恭顺，敬仰

and let me eat you up!" With these words, it pounced on Mr. Dongguo. He was afraid and angry, so he dodged in a panic and avoided the wolf by circling around the donkey.

At this time, there came an old man with a crutch. Mr. Dongguo hurriedly asked the old man to do justice. When the old man heard what had happened, he said to the wolf, "Why did you **betray** the man who had saved your life?" The wolf defended himself, "Don't listen to his nonsense. He just now stuffed me into the bag, tied my hands and feet with ropes, and pressed my body under a pile of books, obviously planning to **suffocate** me in the airtight bag. Shouldn't I eat such a person?"

The old man thought it about and said, "You both have your own reasons, and it is difficult for me to judge. As the saying goes, 'Seeing is believing.' Show me again what happened just now, and I will testify for you. Then you can eat him in peace." The wolf gladly heeded the old man's persuasion, and asked Dongguo to tie its hands and feet and put it back into the book bag. At this point, the old man raised his pigweed staff and struck the wolf severely.

betray
v. 背叛，恩将仇报

suffocate
v. （使）窒息而死

✻ Moral

People should be kind, but they should make a clear distinction between right and wrong rather than show pity on the wolf-like wickedness. "Mr. Dongguo" refers to those who don't tell right from wrong but show pity randomly, while "the Zhongshan Wolf" refers to these who are ungrateful and bite the hand that feeds them.

寓言故事

给猫取名儿

《应谐录》

乔奄家里养了一只猫,自以为非常奇特,就称它为"虎猫"。乔奄经常抱着"虎猫"在人前炫耀。

有一天,他请客人吃饭,又把"虎猫"抱了出来。客人们为了讨好乔奄,争着说好话:"虎虽然勇猛,但是不如龙神奇。我认为应该叫'龙猫'。"

"不妥,不妥。龙虽然神奇,但是没有云气托住,龙升不到天上,所以应该叫'云猫'。"

"云气遮天蔽日,气象不凡,但是一阵狂风就可以把它吹得烟消云散。建议叫它'风猫'。"

"大风确实威力无比,但是一堵墙壁就可以挡住狂风。不如叫'墙猫'。"

"这位的意见我不敢苟同。墙壁对风来说,是可以抵挡一阵,但是跟老鼠一比就不行了。老鼠可以在墙上打洞。请改名为'鼠猫'。"

这时,一位老人站了起来:"你们啊,争奇斗胜,把脑子都搞糊涂了。逮老鼠的是谁?不就是猫嘛!猫就是猫,搞那么多名堂干什么呢!"

【寓意】有一些人,就喜欢图虚名。在一只普普通通的猫身上也要大做文章,弄得自相矛盾,笑话百出,名不副实。做人应该实在些,不要一味地追求形式,要考虑实用性。

Naming Cat for Bubble Reputation

From *Ying Xie Lu*

Qiao Yan had a cat in his family. He thought the cat was extremely extraordinary, so he called it "Tiger Cat". Qiao Yan often held the cat in his arms and **showed off** in front of people.

show off
炫耀

One day, he invited guests to dinner and brought the cat out again. In order to please Mr. Qiao, the guests fought for his favor, saying, "Although a tiger is brave, it is not as magical as a dragon. I think it should be called 'Dragon Cat'."

"It's not appropriate. Although a dragon is magical, it can't fly high in the sky without the supporting from cloud. Thus, it should be called 'Cloud Cat'."

"The cloud covers the sky and blocks out the sun, leading to extraordinary weather, but it could be blown away completely by a gust of wind. It is suggested to call it 'Wind Cat'."

"The wind is indeed incredibly powerful, but a wall can keep it out. We might as well call it 'Wall Cat'."

"I beg to **differ from** this person's opinion. A wall can resist the wind for a while, but it is no match for a mouse. The mouse can make holes in the wall. Please change the name to 'Mouse Cat'."

differ from
区别，不同于

寓言故事

At that moment, an old man stood up and said, "You guys are getting confused by competing with each other. Who is the one that catches a mouse? It's just a cat! A cat is a cat, so what's the point of all these **fusses**!"

fuss

n. 无谓的激动（或忧虑、活动）

Moral

There are some people who like to gain the bubble reputation for themselves. Even over an ordinary cat, they want to make a big fuss, causing **contradictions**, jokes and misrepresentations. We should be honest, not focusing on the outward form but on the inner practicality.

contradiction

n. 不一致，矛盾

公输刻凤

《刘子》

公输班（鲁班）是古代著名的能工巧匠。有一次，他精心刻制一只凤凰。工作才进行到一半，凤冠和凤爪还没有刻完，翠羽也没有披上，旁观的人们就在指指点点，评头论足了。有的指着没有羽毛的凤身，说像一只白毛老鹰；有的摸着没安羽冠的凤头，称它为秃头白鹅。人们都在嘲笑鲁班的笨拙。

鲁班没有理会人们的嘲讽，继续精心雕琢。待到完工的时候，人们简直惊呆了。翠绿的凤冠高高耸立，朱红的凤爪闪闪发亮，全身锦绣般的羽毛像披上了五彩缤纷的霞光，两只美丽的翅膀一张一合像升起了一道道彩虹。鲁班拨动机关，凤凰张开翅膀，在屋梁的上下盘旋翻飞，整整三天不落地面。于是，人们纷纷赞美凤凰的神采，称道鲁班的技艺高超。

【寓意】我们要学会客观、全面地观察问题，不能片面地下结论。

Lu Ban Carving Phoenix

From *Liuzi*

Gongshu Ban (Lu Ban) was a famous craftsman in ancient times. Once upon a time, he carved a phoenix carefully. While it was only halfway through the work, the phoenix crown and claws had not been carved and emerald feathers had not been put on, the people on the sidelines were pointing and commenting. Some pointed to the featherless phoenix and said it was like a white-haired eagle; some touched the head of the phoenix without the feathered crown and called it a bald white goose. People were laughing at Lu Ban's clumsiness.

Ignoring people's ridicule and sarcasm, Lu Ban continued to carve the phoenix meticulously. When it was finished, people were stunned. The phoenix's emerald green crown towered high, its scarlet claws sparkled, its **embroidered** splendid feathers seemed to be covered with a colorful glow, and its two beautiful wings spread like rising rainbows one after another. When Lu Ban plucked the mechanism, the phoenix spread its wings and circled and flipped up and down the house beam, for three whole days without falling to the ground. As a result, people praised the phoenix's presence, and praised Lu Ban's superb skills.

ignore
v. 忽略

embroider
v. 刻

Moral

We must learn to observe issues objectively and comprehensively, and not draw one-sided conclusions.

海龟和群蚁

《符子》

从前,东海有一只大海龟,它能把蓬莱山顶在头上在大海里遨游,上能抵达天际,下可潜入海底。

有一只红蚂蚁听到了关于海龟的传闻,就约了一群蚂蚁,翻山越岭,来到海边,想亲眼看看海龟的本领。

然而,一个多月过去了,却始终不见海龟浮出海面。蚂蚁们不耐烦了,吵着要回老家去。突然风呼海啸,巨浪排空,整个大地都在震动。蚂蚁们齐声嚷嚷:"海龟出海了,海龟出海了!"

大海沸腾了好几天,然后风停了,浪平了,大地也停止了震动。

这时,海里隐约有座山在慢慢地向西移动,顶着这座高山的正是那只神奇的大海龟。

众蚂蚁说:"大海龟顶大山跟咱们顶米粒有什么两样?它顶着大山在海面上游动,咱们顶着米粒在土堆上爬行;它能够潜入海底,咱们能够钻进洞穴。没什么两样,只是表现方式不一样罢了。既然咱们自己就有这样高强的本领,何必翻山越岭来看海龟表演呢?咱们回去吧!"

【寓意】对别人的长处不屑一顾,总自以为是,不是该有的客观态度。

A Sea Turtle and a Group of Ants

From *Fuzi*

Once upon a time, there was a big sea turtle in the East Sea, which could swim in the sea with Mount Penglai on top of its head, jumping up to touch the clouds and diving down to the bottom of the sea.

When a red ant heard the rumor about the turtle, it asked a group of ants to come to the sea, climbing over mountains to see for themselves what the turtle could do.

However, more than a month passed, the turtle did not come to the surface of the sea. The ants got impatient and clamored to go back home. Suddenly the wind **whistled**, the sea roared, giant waves rose and the whole earth shook. The ants shouted in unison, "The sea turtle is out of the sea!"

The sea had **bubbled** like boiled water for several days, then the wind stopped, the waves calmed down, and the earth stopped shaking.

At this time, there seemed to be a faint mountain slowly moving westward in the sea, and it was the big magical turtle that carried the mountain!

The ants said, "What's the difference between the big turtle carrying a mountain and we carrying grains of rice? It swims on the surface of the sea with a big mountain

whistle
v. 吹哨，呼啸

bubble
v. (液体) 冒泡，起泡，沸腾

on its head, and we crawl on the mound of the earth with the grains of rice on our backs; he can dive to the bottom of the sea, and we can burrow into the hole. There is no difference by nature, just difference in the patterns of **manifestation**. Since we have such great skills ourselves, why do we have to cross mountains to see the show of a sea turtle? Let's go back!"

❖ Moral

It is not an objective attitude to despise the strengths of others and to be **self-righteous**, which we should get rid of.

manifestation
n. 表明，表示

self-righteous
adj. 自以为有道理的

海鸟之死

《庄子》

鲁国的郊外飞来了一只奇异的海鸟。人们从来没有见过这种鸟,大家争先恐后地观看。消息传进宫中,鲁王以为神鸟下凡,派人把鸟捉来,亲自迎接供养在庙堂里。

为了表示对海鸟的爱护和尊重,鲁王让宫廷乐队为海鸟演奏庄重肃穆的宫廷音乐,准备最丰盛的筵席款待海鸟。海鸟被这种突如其来的场面和氛围吓得头晕目眩,惊慌失措,一连三天不吃不喝,活活饿死了。

这是以养人的方式养鸟,不是以养鸟的方式养鸟。

【寓意】考虑任何事情要从对方的实际需要出发,而不是从自身的主观愿望出发。鲁王自以为是,好心优待海鸟变成了残酷虐待,最终事与愿违,要了海鸟的性命。

寓言故事

Death of the Seabird

From *Zhuangzi*

In the **outskirts** of Lu State, a strange seabird flew in. People here had never seen this kind of bird before, and they rushed to watch it. When the news reached the palace, the King of Lu State thought it was a divine bird that had come to earth and sent someone to capture the bird. The King greeted it in person and kept it in the temple.

In order to show his love and respect for the seabird, the King of Lu State asked the court band to play **solemn** court music for the seabird and prepare the most **sumptuous** banquet to entertain it. The seabird was so panicked by the sudden scene and atmosphere that it went without eating or drinking for three days in a row and died of starvation.

It is to raise birds by way of raising people instead of raising birds.

outskirts
n. (市镇的) 边缘地带

solemn
adj. 庄严的

sumptuous
adj. 华贵的，奢华的

❀ Moral

When we do things, we need to take into account the actual needs of the other party instead of our own wishes. The King's self-righteous kindness to the seabird turned into cruelty and mistreatment, which eventually **backfired** and killed the seabird.

backfire
v. 产生事与愿违的不良后果

河豚发怒

《柳河东集》

有一种鱼叫河豚,小脑袋、大肚子,喜欢在木桥的柱子之间游来游去。

一天,风和日丽,河豚边唱歌边游泳,不小心一头撞在桥柱子上。河豚顿时怒发冲冠,无论如何也不肯离开,要和柱子讲道理。

河豚质问柱子为什么要撞自己?它生气的时候,两腮张开了,身上的鳍也竖起来了,鼓起肚子,浮在水面上,瞪着血红的眼睛,要柱子给它一个说法。

这时候,有只老鹰飞来,伸出利爪,一把抓住圆鼓鼓的河豚,撕裂了它的肚皮,把它吃掉了。

【寓意】遇事不冷静,后果很严重。

Globefish Getting Very Angry

From *Anthology of Liu Hedong*

There was a fish with small head and big belly, being called **globefish**, and it liked to swim between the pillars of a wooden bridge.

One day, the sun shining, the globefish accidentally bumped into a bridge pillar while it was singing and swimming. The fish suddenly became so angry that it refused to leave and tried to reason with the pillar.

The globefish asked why the pillar struck him. When the fish got angry, it opened its gills, **erected** its fins, bulged its belly, floated on the surface of the water, glared with its blood shot eyes and asked for an explanation from the pillar.

At that time, an eagle flew in, reached out its sharp claws, grabbing the **bulbous** globefish, ripping its belly, and eating it up.

❧ Moral

If we don't keep calm in case of trouble, there will be serious consequences.

---

globefish

n. 河豚，刺鲀

erect

v. 竖起

bulbous

adj. 鳞茎状的

涸辙之鱼

《庄子》

战国时期，庄子家里很穷，已经两天揭不开锅了，他只好去向监河侯借粮。

监河侯吝啬又狡猾，他对庄子说："好啊！等我从老百姓那儿收到租子后，就借给你三百两黄金，怎么样？"

庄子听他这么说，气得脸色煞白，忿忿地说："来的路上我听到呼救的声音，寻声找去，看到车轮碾出的泥沟里有一条鲫鱼，正大张着嘴对我喘气。我问它：'鲫鱼呀，你是哪里来的？'它回答：'我是东海海神的臣子。今天落在这条干枯的车轮沟里，快渴死了，你能给我点凉水，救我一命吗？'我说：'好啊！我正要到南方去拜见吴王、越王，请他们把西江的水引过来救你，你看可以吗？'鲫鱼生气地说：'我失去了水，没有安身的地方。我现在只需要一点点水，就能活命，你却说了这么一大堆不着边际的废话。你不用再说了，干脆直接到干鱼摊上找我吧！'"

【寓意】"涸辙之鱼"比喻在困境中亟待救援的人。远水解不了近渴，这是常识。这则故事揭露了监河侯假大方、真吝啬的伪善面目，讽刺了说大话空话，不解决实际问题之人。

Fish Stranded in Dry Rut

From *Zhuangzi*

During the Warring States Period, Zhuangzi's family was so poor that they had not made ends meet for two days. Thus, Zhuangzi had no choice but to borrow grain and rice from a **marquis**, an official who was responsible for managing rivers.

marquis

n. 侯爵

The marquis, both stingy and cunning, said to Zhuangzi, "Well, after I collect the rent from civilians, how about lending you three hundred taels of gold?"

When Zhuangzi heard, his face turned pale with anger. He said **vehemently**, "On my way here, I heard a cry for help. When I looked for the cry, I saw a crucian carp in the mud ditch that had been run over by a wheel, gasping for breath in front of me with its mouth wide open. I asked, 'Crucian carp, where are you from?' It answered, 'I am a courtier of the Sea God from the East Sea. Today, I fell in the dry rut, dying of thirst. Could you please give me some cold water, so as to save my life?' I replied, 'With pleasure, I'm going to the south to meet the two kings of Wu State and Yue State. Then I will ask them to bring some water from the West River, so as to save you. Do you think that's all right?' The fish said violently, 'Without water, I don't have a place to stay and can't survive. All

vehemently

adv. 忿忿地

I need now is only a little bit of water to stay alive, but you're saying a bunch of nonsense. You don't have to say this any more, just go straight to the dried fish stall to look for me.' "

Moral

"Fish stranded in a dry rut" is a metaphor, used to describe a person in a desperate situation and in dire need of help. It is a common sense that distant water cannot **quench** immediate thirst. The story exposes the hypocritical and miserly marquis, and **satirizes** the usual tricks of those who lie and talk empty words without solving real problems.

quench
v. 解（渴），止（渴）

satirize
v. 讽刺

后羿射箭

《苻子》

历史上有两位后羿。一位生于尧帝时代，有"后羿射日"的故事；一位生于夏朝时代，有"后羿射箭"的故事。

有一天，夏王让后羿表演箭术。靶子是用一尺见方的兽皮制成的，正中画了直径为一寸的红心，作为靶心。后羿微微一笑，毫不在意。

临射前，夏王突然宣布："射中了靶心，赏你一万两黄金；射不中，就剥夺你拥有的封地。"后羿听了，顿时紧张起来，脸色一阵红一阵白，胸脯一起一伏，怎么也平静不下来。就这样，他拉开了弓，射出第一支箭，没有中。射出了第二支箭，又没有中。

夏王问大臣弥仁："后羿平时射箭是百发百中的，为什么今天连射两箭都脱靶了呢？"

弥仁说："后羿是被患得患失的情绪害了。大王定下的赏罚条件成了他的包袱，所以他的表现得很不正常。如果人们能够抛弃患得患失的情绪，把厚赏重罚置之度外，再加上刻苦训练，那么普天下的人都不会比后羿差的。"

【寓意】保持平常心，不要因为患得患失的心态影响自己能力的发挥，也就是说，不要为金钱名利之类的身外之物所累。

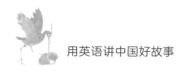

Hou Yi Shooting Arrows

From *Fuzi*

There were two great men named Hou Yi in history. One was born during the period of Emperor Yao, and had the story of "Hou Yi shooting down nine suns"; the other was born in the Xia Dynasty, and had the story of "Hou Yi shooting arrows".

One day, the Emperor of Xia Dynasty asked Hou Yi to perform archery. The target was made of a one-foot square piece of animal skin, with a one-inch-diameter red heart painted in the center as the bull's-eye. Hou Yi smiled and didn't care.

Just before shooting, the Emperor suddenly announced, "Hit the bull's-eye, and I will **reward** you ten thousand taels of gold; miss it, and I will **deprive of** your fiefdom." On hearing the Emperor's words, Hou Yi became nervous instantly, his face flushing, and his chest rising and falling and he could not calm down at all. He drew his bow and shot the first arrow, but missed. So was the second time.

The Emperor asked his official Mi Ren, "Hou Yi is an archery expert, usually shooting a hundred arrows without a single miss, but why did he miss twice today?"

Mi Ren explained, "Hou Yi was influenced by the

reward
v. 奖励

deprive of
剥夺

emotion of worrying about gain and loss. The conditions of reward and punishment set by you became a burden to him, so he performed abnormally. If people can abandon the mood of worrying about gain and loss, put aside heavy reward and punishment, coupled with hard training, no one in the world will be worse than the archery expert Hou Yi."

❖ Moral

Keep a normal state of mind, and don't let the sense of worrying about gain and loss affect your ability to perform. That is to say, don't be burdened by such money, fame or wealth.

糊涂的麋鹿

《柳河东集》

临江有个猎人,捉到一只还在吃奶的小麋鹿。他十分爱怜这只温顺的小动物,决定抱回家中饲养。

猎人刚跨进家门,十几条猎狗就一拥而上,目露凶光,口流涎水,想吃小麋鹿。猎人大怒,棒打脚踢,把猎狗狠狠地教训了一顿。为了增进猎狗和麋鹿之间的感情,猎人就每天抱着小麋鹿到狗群中去,让它们相互熟悉。只要哪只猎狗稍稍流露一点不良的意图,猎人立刻就把它毒打一顿。时间一久,小麋鹿跟这群猎狗混熟了。它们经常在一起玩耍,追逐打滚,十分亲昵。

这些猎狗虽然很想尝尝鲜嫩的鹿肉,但是惧怕主人的鞭子,只能把唾沫往肚子里咽。小麋鹿仗着主人的保护,得意忘形,忘了狗是自己的天敌,反而把猎狗当成好伙伴。

三年后的一天,小麋鹿自个儿跑到大门外去玩耍。它看见远处有一群狗在追逐嬉闹,立刻跑进狗群跟它们一起玩耍。

这群猎狗发现了小麋鹿,立即猛扑了上来,很快把小麋鹿吃了。可怜的小麋鹿到死也没有弄明白,为什么朋友一下子变成了凶残的敌人。

【寓意】看人看事,一定不要被假象所迷惑,要深入观察、分析,准确地把握它的实质,从而分清是非善恶,采取正确的态度和处理方法。

A Muddled Elk

From *Anthology of Liu Hedong*

There was a hunter in Linjiang, who caught a baby elk that was still suckling. He pitied and loved the little gentle animal so much that he decided to take it home to raise.

As soon as the hunter stepped into his house, more than a dozen of hounds **swarmed over** him, **salivating** and trying to eat the little elk with fierce looks on their faces. The hunter was furious, and gave the hounds a good lesson by beating and kicking them. In order to improve the relationship between the hounds and the elk, the hunter carried the young elk to the hounds every day so that they could get to know each other better. If any of the hounds showed the slightest bad intention, the hunter would immediately beat them up. As time went by, the little elk got acquainted with the herd of hunting dogs. The elk and hounds often played together, chased and rolled around, and became very intimate.

Although these hounds wanted to taste the tender venison, they could only swallow the spittle into their stomachs for fear of the master's whip. The little elk, on the other hand, relied on the master's protection, forgot that the hounds were its natural enemies, and regarded them as its good companions.

swarm over

成群结队地走过

salivate

v. 垂涎，流口水

One day three years later, the little elk ran outside the gate to play. When the elk saw a pack of dogs chasing and playing in the distance, it immediately ran into the pack to play with them.

These dogs found the elk, immediately pounced on it and instantly ate it. Until its death, the poor little elk didn't understand why these "friendly" hounds suddenly turned into **ferocious** enemies.

ferocious

adj. 凶残的，凶猛的

❋ Moral

When looking at people and things, we must not be confused by illusions, but observe, analyze, and accurately grasp the very essence, so as to distinguish between right and wrong, good and evil, and adopt the correct attitude and method of handling them.

寓言故事

画鬼最易

《韩非子》

春秋时期,有位画家被齐王请来为自己画像。

齐王问画家:"比较起来,什么东西最难画呢?"

画家回答:"活动的狗与马是最难画的。"

齐王又问:"画什么最容易呢?"

画家说:"画鬼最容易。"

"为什么呢?"齐王好奇地问。

"因为狗与马这些动物,人人都熟悉,天天能看见,哪怕画错一点点,任何人都能指出来。至于鬼呢,就不一样了,谁也没见过,无影无形,任凭我怎么画,谁也不能证明我画得不像,所以画鬼最容易。"

【寓意】胡编乱造,胡写乱画,这是很简单的事;但要真正认识客观事物,并恰如其分地表现它,就不是一件容易事了。

Easiest to Draw Ghosts

From *Hanfeizi*

During the Spring and Autumn Period, a painter was invited by the King of Qi State to paint his portrait.

The King asked the painter, "In comparison, what is the most difficult thing to paint?"

The painter replied, "The dogs and horses in motion are the most difficult to paint."

The King asked, "What is the easiest to paint?"

The painter said, "It's easiest to draw ghosts."

"Why?" the King questioned curiously.

"Because such animals as dogs and horses are familiar to everyone, and can be observed every day, anyone can point out even the slightest mistake. As for ghosts, no one has ever seen them, which are different from dogs and horses. So it's easiest to draw ghosts."

Moral

It is a very simple thing to make up and scribble **at will**, but it is not an easy task to truly understand objective things and express them appropriately.

at will
随心所欲

纪昌学射

《列子》

古时候,有位射箭能手叫甘蝇,他只要一拉弓,射兽兽倒,射鸟鸟落,百发百中。飞卫是甘蝇的学生,射箭的本领超过了老师甘蝇。

有一个名叫纪昌的人,拜飞卫为师学射箭。飞卫对纪昌说:"你先学会看东西不眨眼睛,然后才可以学射箭。"

纪昌回到家里,仰面躺在他妻子的织布机下,两眼一眨不眨地盯着织布机上的梭子练习。这样坚持练了两年,从不间断,即使有人拿锥子向他眼睛刺去,他也不眨一下眼睛。纪昌高兴地向师傅飞卫汇报自己的训练成果。飞卫说:"仅有这点本领还不行,你要练出好眼力,练到极小的东西你能看得很大,模糊的东西你能看得一清二楚。有了这样的本领,再来告诉我。"

纪昌又回到家里,选一根最细的牦牛尾巴上的毛,一端系上一个小虱子,另一端悬挂在自家的窗口上,两眼注视着吊在窗口牦牛毛下端的小虱子,天天目不转睛地看着。十多天过去了,那虱子因为风干了,所以显得更加细小,但在纪昌眼里慢慢地大起来,越来越清晰。这样练了三年,这只小虱子在他眼里竟有车轮那么大。这个时候,纪昌再看其他的东西,简直大得像小山似的,又大又清晰。于是,纪昌拉弓搭箭,向虱子射去,箭头竟然从虱子的中心穿过,而悬挂虱子的牦牛毛却没有被碰到。纪昌这才深深体会到师傅的良苦用心,马上向飞卫汇报自己的成绩和心得。

飞卫听后,为纪昌高兴,笑着说:"功夫不负有心人,你成功了!"

【寓意】好本领是苦练出来的。在良师的引导下,刻苦学习,持之以恒,终能成功。

Ji Chang Learning Archery

From *Liezi*

In ancient times, there was an archery expert named Gan Ying. As long as he drew his bow, he could shoot beasts and birds down without any missing. Fei Wei was Gan Ying's student, whose archery surpassed his teacher's.

There was a man named Ji Chang, who **worshipped** Fei Wei as an apprentice and learned archery from him. Fei Wei told Ji Chang, "You must learn to see targets without blinking before learning to shoot arrows."

Ji Chang went home and lay on his back under his wife's **loom**, staring unblinkingly at the shuttle of the loom. He practiced like this for two years without stop, and even if someone stabbed him in the eye with an awl, he could not blink. Then, Ji Chang happily reported his training results to his master, Fei Wei. Fei Wei said, "The skill is not enough. You have to practice good eyesight so that you can see the 'big objects' that are very small in fact, and see 'clear-cut objects' that are very blurry in fact. Once you have such an aptitude, come back and tell me."

When Ji Chang returned home again, he chose the finest hair from a yak's tail, tied a small louse on one end and hung the other end from the window of his house, and watched the louse hanging at the bottom of the yak hair

worship
v. 崇拜

loom
n. 织布机

with both eyes. More than ten days later, the louse became smaller and smaller because it had dried up, but it became bigger and bigger, clearer and clearer in Ji Chang's eyes. After three years of practice, the louse seemed to be as big as a wheel in his eyes. At this time, when Ji Chang looked at other objects, they were similar to small mountains, big and clear. When Ji Chang drew his bow and shot an arrow at the louse, the arrow passed through the center of the louse without touching the yak hair on which it hung. Only then did Ji Chang deeply appreciate the good intentions of his master. He immediately reported his achievement and experience to Fei Wei.

After hearing this, Fei Wei was happy for Ji Chang and said with a smile, "Where there's a will, there's a way. You've succeeded!"

Moral

Good skills come from hard work. Under the guidance of a good teacher, we can succeed with **diligence** and perseverance.

diligence

n. 勤劳

用英语讲中国好故事

击邻家之子

《墨子》

墨子是战国时期墨家学派的创始人。他主张"兼爱非攻",强烈反对战争,因为战争使社会动荡,使人们生活痛苦不堪。墨子有很多学生,他非常重视向学生传授反战思想。

据说,墨子讲课总是深入浅出,用故事说明道理。他曾经向学生讲了这么一个故事:

有位父亲,看到自己的儿子做事强横,也不成器,感到很失望。平时和颜悦色地和儿子讲道理,儿子总是听不进去,实在无计可施,就拿起鞭子教训儿子。这时,他的邻居看见了,也举起棒子来打,边打还边说:"我打你,是顺着你父亲的意愿,帮你父亲教训你。"

故事讲完了,学生们认为这位邻居多管闲事,别人教训孩子,关你什么事。墨子见学生们议论纷纷,接着说道:"邻居这样做固然荒唐无理,可是有些好战的国家也像这个邻居一样,好管闲事,别国的事情总想插手,动不动就以此为借口,向邻国发动战争,这不是无理取闹吗?"

学生们这才明白老师的意思。

【寓意】有些人总是打着冠冕堂皇的理由,干涉他人。这则寓言讽刺了打着漂亮幌子而侵犯人家的无理行为。它体现了墨子的"非攻"思想。

Beating up Neighbor's Son

From *Mozi*

Mozi was the founder of the Mohism in the Warring States Period. He advocated "Universal Love and Non-aggression", and strongly opposed war which caused social unrest and misery to people. Mozi had many students and placed great importance on imparting the anti-war ideas to students.

It is said that Mozi explained profound theories in simple words, with stories to illustrate the truth. Once he told such a story to his students:

There was a father who was disappointed at his son, **overbearing** and incompetent. Usually, he, with a pleasant face, reasoned with his son, but his son never listened. He really could not think of any method, he picked up a whip and struck his son, so as to teach him a lesson. At that time, one of his neighbors saw and raised a stick and hit him, saying, "I beat you at your father's pleasure, to help him teach you a lesson."

The story being finished, the students thought that the neighbor was meddling in other people's business. When Mozi saw that his students had a lot to say, he said, "It is certainly absurd and unreasonable for a neighbor to do this, but some warlike countries behaved just like this neighbor,

overbearing
adj. 专横的

meddling in other countries' affairs, always wanting to **interfere**, and using this as an excuse to start wars against their neighbors at every turn. Isn't it unreasonable?"

Only then did the students understand what their teacher meant.

❖ Moral

There are always some people who interfere with others under the pretext of high-sounding reasons. The fable satirizes the unreasonable behaviors of those who violate others under the guise of pretty **camouflages**. It embodies Mozi's idea of "Non-aggression".

interfere
v. 干涉

camouflage
n. 伪装

棘刺尖儿上雕猴子

《韩非子》

  燕王到处张贴榜文，征求身怀绝技的能工巧匠。有个卫国人来应征，自称能在荆棘的尖刺上雕刻出活灵活现的猴子。燕王听说他有这样超群的技艺，高兴极了，立刻给他极其丰厚的待遇，供养在身边。

  过了几天，燕王想看看这位巧匠雕刻的艺术珍品。那个卫国人说："国君要是想看的话，还请依我两个条件：一是半年之内不入后宫与后妃欢聚；二是不喝酒不吃肉。然后选一个雨停日出的天气，在半明半暗的光线中，才能看到我在棘刺尖儿上雕刻的猴子。"

  燕王一听这些条件，没法照办，只能继续用锦衣玉食把这个卫国人供养在内宫，却始终没有机会欣赏到他刻制的珍品。

  宫内有个铁匠听说了这件事，不禁暗暗发笑。他对燕王说："我是专门打制刀具的。谁都知道，再小的刻制品也要用刻刀才能雕出来，所以雕刻的东西一定要比刻刀的刀刃大。如果棘刺的尖儿细到容不下最小的刀刃，那就没法在上面雕刻。请国王检查一下那位工匠的刻刀，就可以知道他说的话是真是假了。"

  大王一听，如梦方醒，立即把那个卫国人找来，问道："你在棘刺尖儿上雕刻猴子，用的是什么工具？"

  卫国人回答："刻刀。"

  燕王说："请把你的刻刀拿给我看看。"

  卫国人一听就慌了神，借口说到住处去取刻刀，然后溜出宫门逃跑了。

【寓意】谎言编得再巧妙，也经不住分析、考察，经不住实践检验。根据这则寓言故事，后人常常把谎言称为"棘刺之说"。

Monkey Carved on the Thorn Tip

From *Hanfeizi*

The King of Yan State put up posters everywhere, looking for skilled craftsmen. There was a man from Wei State who applied for the position, claiming that he could carve monkeys on the tips of thorns. The King of Yan was so delighted to hear of his outstanding skills that he immediately offered him a generous salary and made him stay in the palace.

After a few days, the King wanted to see the artistic treasures carved by this **ingenious** craftsman. The craftsman said, "If you would like to see it, please follow my two conditions: First, you must not enter your imperial harem to reunite with your concubines for half a year; second, you must not drink wine or eat meat. Then choose a rainy day when the sun rises, in half-light and half-darkness, so that you could see the monkeys I carved on the thorn tip."

Upon hearing these conditions, the King of Yan could not comply with them, so he had to continue to treat this craftsman in the palace with fine clothes and delicious food. However, he never got a chance to **appreciate** the treasures carved by him.

When a blacksmith in the palace heard about it, he

ingenious
adj. 有天赋的

appreciate
v. 欣赏

could not help laughing secretly. He said, "I am a specialist in making knives. Everyone knows that even the smallest **engraved** object can only be carved with a carving knife, so the carving must be larger than the blade of the knife. If the tip of thorns is so thin that it can't accommodate the smallest blade, you won't be possible to carve on it. Please ask to examine the craftsman's carving knife, and you will know whether what he said is true or false."

Upon hearing it, the King, as if wakened from a dream, immediately called the man of Wei and asked, "What tool did you use to carve the monkey on the tip of thorns?"

The man replied, "A carving knife."

The King said, "Please show me your carving knife."

On hearing it, the man panicked and, on the pretext of going to his residence to fetch his carving knife, slipped out of the palace gate and took to his heels.

❖ Moral

No matter how skillfully a lie is made up, it cannot stand the analysis and investigation, nor the test of practice. According to the fable, lies are often called "words of the thorn tips".

---

engrave

v. 雕刻

姜从树生

《雪涛小说》

从前,有个楚国人没有见过生姜。一天,他骑着毛驴进城,看到有人在卖生姜,很是好奇,就在一旁观看。然后,他对身旁的人说:"这东西一定是从树上结出来的。"

身旁有人告诉他:"你说错了,这东西是从土里长成的。"

楚国人坚持自己的看法,说:"我们一起找十个人来问,我愿意拿我乘坐的毛驴作赌注。"

他们一共问了十个人,都说生姜是从土里长成的。这个楚国人哑口无言,面色苍白,又固执地说:"毛驴就给你了,但生姜还是从树上长出来的。"

【寓意】不懂不要装懂,要虚心求教,知错就改。固执己见,就会贻笑大方。这则寓言讽刺了那些因爱面子而固执己见的人。

寓言故事

Ginger Growing on Trees

From *Xuetao Novel*

Once upon a time, there was a man of Chu State who had never seen ginger. One day, he rode into town on a donkey and saw some selling ginger, so he felt very **curious** and watched from the sidelines. Then he said to the people next to him, "It must come from a tree."

Someone beside him told, "You're wrong. It grows in the soil."

The man insisted on his opinion and said, "Let's ask ten people together, and I'm willing to **bet** the donkey I'm riding on."

They asked ten people in all, and were told in a consistent manner that ginger grew in the soil. The man of Chu was dumb with a pale face, and stubbornly said, "You can have the donkey, but the ginger still grows on the tree."

curious

adj. 好奇的

bet

v. 用……打赌

🌀 Moral

We should not pretend to know what we don't really know. We should seek advice with an open mind and correct our mistakes. Persisting in our opinions blindly will expose us to ridicule. This story satirizes those who cling to their own opinions because of face-saving.

匠石运斤

《庄子》

庄子去送葬,路过惠子的墓地,回头对跟从者说:"郢都有个粉刷匠,整天辛苦地为人粉刷屋子,常常弄得自己满脸满身灰尘。有一天,他照镜子时发现自己鼻尖上多了一块白泥,那白泥像蚊蝇的翅膀那样又细又薄,怎么也抠不下来,仿佛长在鼻尖上。粉刷匠非常苦恼,于是便向他的好朋友石匠求助。石匠挥起斧子像一阵风似的,将石灰都砍掉了而鼻子完好无损。整个过程中,粉刷匠站在那里一动不动,面不改色。宋元君听说了这件事,觉得不可思议,便召见石匠进宫表演给他看。石匠说:'我曾经的确能够砍掉鼻尖上的白泥,但那位信任我让我砍的粉刷匠朋友已经死去很久了。'自从惠子先生死后,便没有跟我谈论道理的人了!"

【寓意】"匠石运斤"形容技艺精湛超群。成功是相互合作的结果,相互间的信任是合作成功的关键。没有信任作为前提,仅有高超的技艺也无能为力。

 寓言故事

Stonemason Wielding Axe

From *Zhuangzi*

When Zhuangzi attended a burial ceremony, he passed by Huizi's graveyard, turned back and said to his followers, "There is a whitewasher in Yingdu, whitewashing houses for other people all day long and often getting dust all over his face. One day, looking in the mirror, he found a piece of lime **slurry** on the tip of his nose, which was as thin as the wings of a mosquito or a fly. He could not get it off. It was like growing on the tip of nose. The whitewasher was very **distressed**, and asked for help from his good friend, a stonecutter. The stonecutter swung his axe like a gust of wind and chopped off all the lime, leaving the nose intact. During the whole process, the whitewasher stood there, not moving a step but keeping calm. When the King Yuan of Song State heard about the incident, he thought it incredible, so he **summoned** the stonecutter into the palace to show him how it was done. The stonemason said, 'I was once indeed able to cut off the white slurry on the nose tip, but my friend, the whitewasher, who trusted me to cut it off, had died a long time ago.' Since the death of Huizi, there has been no one to talk about reasons with me!"

slurry

n. 泥浆，稀泥

distressed

adj. 苦恼的

summon

v. 召唤，传唤

Moral

The fable is used to describe a man of superb skills. Success is the result of mutual cooperation, and the key to successful cooperation is mutual trust. Without trust as a **prerequisite**, the one with mere superb skills cannot do anything to help.

prerequisite
n. 前提

寓言故事

狡生梦金

《雪涛小说》

从前,有个书生喜欢说谎话。他在私塾读书时,就骗过先生。先生平时管教严厉,谁要犯错了就得挨板子。

有一天,这个书生违反了规定,先生大怒,派人把学生找来,要严加惩罚。学生来了后,突然跪倒在先生脚下,说:"学生我偶然得到一千金正忙着处理,所以迟到了,请先生您原谅。"先生听到学生得了那么多金子,羡慕又好奇地问:"你从哪里得到的?"学生说:"从地里挖到的。"先生更加好奇,接着问:"你打算怎样处理这些金子?"学生回答说:"我家里非常贫穷,我同妻子商量,打算用五百金买田地,二百金买房产,一百金买器具,一百金买僮仆和婢妾。还剩下一百金,用其中的一半买书,从今以后发愤读书,另一半送给先生,以报答您平日教育我的恩德。"先生听了大喜过望,说:"我怎么担当得起啊?谢谢你心里还想着先生。中午我请客,你我师生畅饮一番。"

席间,先生请书生坐下,还主动给书生敬酒。酒到兴头,先生问学生:"你刚才说得了一千金,这些金子可都收藏好了?"书生站起来回答说:"我把这些金子的用途刚计划好,就被老婆一个转身把我碰醒了。梦醒了,金子也就没有了。"先生一听,惊愕地问道:"你是说做梦梦见金子了?"书生回答:"的确是在做梦。"先生很不高兴,又不好发怒,言不由衷地说:"你对我还是有情意的,就连梦里得了金子也不忘记为师。"

【寓意】先生本来要严肃纪律,教训学生,却被学生花言巧语骗了。莫不是他心里贪财,又怎么会受此愚弄?最后,不但没得到钱财,还丢了师德。

Sly Student Dreaming about Gold

From *Xuetao Novel*

Once upon a time, there was a student who liked to tell lies. When he was studying in a private school, he often lied to his teacher. However, the teacher was usually serious about discipline, and anyone who made mistakes would have to be **reprimanded** with a board.

One day, the student **violated** the regulations, and the teacher was **furious** and sent for the student to be severely punished. On arriving, the student suddenly knelt down by the teacher's feet and said, "I accidentally got one thousand taels of gold and was busy dealing with it, so I was late. Please forgive me, teacher." When the teacher heard that the student had gotten so much gold, he asked with envy and curiosity, "Where did you get it?" The student said, "I dug it out of the ground." The teacher became more curious and then asked, "What are you going to do with it?" The student replied, "My family is very poor, so I have discussed with my wife that I planned to use five hundred taels of gold to buy land, two hundred taels of gold to buy real estate, one hundred taels of gold to buy **utensils**, and one hundred taels of gold to buy servants and maids as well as concubines. There is still one hundred taels of gold left, and I will use half of it to buy books so that I can

reprimand
v. 训斥
violate
v. 违反
furious
adj. 狂怒的

utensil
n. 器具，家什

study with great enthusiasm from now on. As for the other half, it will be given to you, sir, in return for your kindness in educating me on weekdays." Hearing this, the teacher was **overjoyed** and said, "How can I afford to accept it? Thank you for thinking of me in your heart. I will treat you at noon, and we will have a drink."

During the dinning, the teacher invited his student to sit down and offered him a toast. When they drank happily, the teacher asked his student, "You just said you got one thousand taels of gold. Have you hidden all of them?" The student stood up and replied, "After I had just planned out what I was going to do with the gold, my wife turned around and woke me up. When I woke up from my dream, the gold was gone." Upon hearing this, the teacher asked in **consternation**, "You mean you dreamed about gold?" The student replied, "It was indeed a dream." Quite unhappy but unable to get angry, the teacher said insincerely, "You still have affection for me, and you did not forget me, your teacher, even when you got gold in your dream."

overjoyed
adj. 大喜过望的；欣喜若狂的

consternation
n. 惊愕

❖ **Moral**

The teacher was supposed to be serious about discipline and teach his student a lesson, but he was deceived by his student's sweet words. If he had not been greedy for money in his heart, how could he be fooled like this? At last, the teacher not only got no money, but also lost his virtues as a teacher.

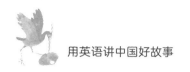

截竿进城

《笑林》

鲁国有个人,扛着一根又粗又长的竹竿进城。到了城门口,他把竹竿竖立起来拿着,被城门卡住了;他又把竹竿横过来拿着,又被两边的城墙卡住了。他折腾了半天,累得气喘吁吁,还是进不了城。

不久,有个白胡子老人经过,说:"我不是最有学识的人,只是见得比较多。你为什么不用锯子将竹竿从中截断呢?"于是那个鲁国人依言借了把锯子,把竹竿锯断,拿进城去了。

【寓意】持长竿进城的鲁人头脑简单,做事死板不知变通,但自作聪明、好为人师的白胡子老头更让人可笑,以老资格自居,出馊主意。虚心求教的人同样也应积极动脑筋,绝不能盲目地听从别人的建议。

Entering the City Gate with a Long Pole

From *Xiaolin*

A man of Lu State carried a long, thick bamboo pole and wanted to enter a town. When he arrived at the gate of the town, he held it **upright** and got stuck at the gate; then he held it **horizontally** and got stuck at the walls on both sides. He had the pole adjusted for a long time, tired and out of breath, but he still could not enter the town.

Before long, an old man with the white beard passed by and said, "I'm not the most knowledgeable, but experienced enough. Why don't you use a saw to cut the bamboo pole off in the middle?" The man of Lu State borrowed a saw, as he was told, cut the pole in the middle and carried it into the town.

Moral

The man of Lu State entering the city gate with a long pole was simple-minded and stubborn, but the old man with the white beard who loved to be a teacher of others and fancied himself clever, was even more ridiculous, claiming to be a senior and giving a bad idea. An open-minded person should also run his head actively and never blindly follow the advice of others.

upright
adv. 竖起地
horizontally
adv. 水平地

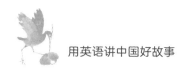

荆人夜涉

《吕氏春秋》

　　古时候，有一回楚国想偷袭宋国，而澭水是夜袭宋国的天然障碍。为了越过障碍，楚国派人先逐段测量澭水的深度，选择一处最浅的水域，并做好了夜间涉水过河的标记。谁知到了夜里，澭水水位突然暴涨。但楚国人不知道，仍旧按照原先设下的标记在深更半夜偷渡。

　　结果，渡河的一千多名士兵全部被激流卷走了。楚军惊恐万状。

【寓意】河水会涨也会落，事物都处在运动变化之中。不研究新情况，不随机应变，仍然依照老办法，肯定不能达到预期结果。

寓言故事

Chu Troop Wading Across River at Night

From *Master Lü's Spring and Autumn Annals*

Once upon a time, Chu State planned to secretly attack Song State. The Yong River was the natural barrier against its surprise attack at night. To **overcome** this obstacle, the Chu people secretly measured depth of the Yong River one section by one section, chose the shallowest one and made marks for **wading** across the river at night. Unexpectedly, when night came, the Yong River suddenly swelled up. Yet, the Chu's army didn't notice and continued with their moving to cross the river according to the original marks they made in the daytime.

As a result, over 1,000 soldiers crossing the river were all **swept away** by the torrent. The Chu's army was terrified.

overcome
v. 克服

wade
v. 涉，蹚（水或淤泥等）

sweep away
消除

◆ Moral

Everything is in motion and changes just as the river rises and falls. If we do not study the new situation and adapt to it, we will certainly not achieve the desired results by following the same old methods.

客套误事

《应谐录》

于啴子跟朋友坐在炉子跟前烤火。朋友靠在桌子上专心看书,长衫的下摆被火烤着了也没有发觉。

于啴子站起身来慢条斯理地抱拳作揖:"适才有件事情想告诉您,因您是急性子,怕您生气伤了身体;想不告诉您吧,又觉得对朋友不负责任。请您答应我,您宽容大度,决不发怒,我才敢奉告。"

朋友说:"您有什么事情尽管说,我一定虚心听取您的意见。"

于啴子像刚才那样谦让,又来一次。到了第三次,他才不紧不慢地说:"刚才炉火烧着您的衣服了。"

朋友一看,衣服下摆已经被烧掉了好大一块。朋友的脸都气白了,说:"你为什么不早点告诉我,这样的事情还啰嗦什么?!"

于啴子反而得了理似的,说:"你看你看,刚才你可是亲口答应不生气的。真是江山易改,本性难移啊!"

【寓意】讲究文明礼貌固然是必要的,但是,一味追求虚礼俗套就会误事。

False Etiquette Spoiling Affairs

From *Ying Xie Lu*

Yu Chanzi and his friend sat in front of a stove to warm themselves. Leaning against the table, his friend **concentrated on** reading books and did not notice that the hem of his own gown was burnt by the fire.

Yu Chanzi stood up and bowed slowly with both hands clasped in front, "I want to tell you something just now, and I am afraid that you will get angry and harm your health since you are hotheaded; if I do not tell you, I will feel irresponsible to you as a friend. Please promise me that you are tolerant and will never get angry before I dare to tell you."

His friend said, "If you have anything to say, I will definitely listen to your advice humbly."

Yu Chanzi was as humble as he was just now and did it again. It was the third time that he had **nonchalantly** said, "Just now the fire burned your clothes."

When his friend had a look, a large **chunk** of the lower part of his clothes had been burned off. His friend, face turning pale with anger, said, "Why didn't you tell me earlier? Why were you so wordy about such a thing?"

concentrate on

聚精会神

nonchalantly

adv. 漫不经心地

chunk

n. 厚块,大块

On the contrary, Yu Chanzi seemed to get a valid point and said, "Look, just now you personally promised not to be angry. It is really true that a leopard can't change its spots!"

Moral

It's important to pay attention to civilization and politeness, but blindly pursuing false etiquette and stereotype will lead to mistakes.

孔雀爱尾

《纪闻》

罗州的山中有很多孔雀,几十只为一群在一起飞翔。

雌孔雀尾巴短,也没有金翠色;雄孔雀出生三年,开始长出小尾巴,五年长成大尾巴。雄孔雀的尾巴金黄、翠绿,画家们用彩笔也描绘不出来。

雄孔雀生性嫉妒,因为自己有美丽的尾巴,总是感到不可一世,看见穿着华丽衣服的小孩,一定会追上去啄他们,仿佛别人都不应该美丽。在山里休息的时候,首先要选择好地方来安放自己的尾巴,然后才安置自己的身体。

有一天,突然下起大雨,有一只雄孔雀的尾巴淋湿了,当伙伴们起飞时,它待在原地,一点也没有要飞的意思。伙伴们催促它:"捕鸟人就要来了,赶快飞走吧!"雄孔雀说:"我的尾巴被雨打湿了,现在我不能飞,不然我漂亮的尾巴就会损坏了,那样我就不美了。"

不一会儿,捕鸟人就到了,这只爱惜尾巴的雄孔雀被抓住了。

【寓意】这则寓言告诫人们,对自己的优点不能看得太重,否则会成为自己的负担,甚至招来杀身之祸。

用英语讲中国好故事

Peacocks Cherishing Their Tails

From *Documentary Stories*

There were many peacocks in the mountains of Luozhou Prefecture, and dozens of them flew together in a flock.

There, female peacocks had short tails with no golden **emerald** color; three years after their birth male peacocks began to grow small tails, and five years later they grew big tails. The male peacock's tail was golden and green, and painters could not paint it even with colored brushes.

Male peacocks were envious by nature, for they had beautiful tails and always felt **superior**. When they saw children dressed in gorgeous clothes, they would certainly catch up with them and peck them, as if no one else should be beautiful. When resting in the mountains, they must first choose a good place to place their tails before placing their bodies.

One day, when it suddenly began to rain heavily, a male peacock got its tail wet, and when its companions took off, it stayed where it was and had no intention of flying. The companions urged it, "The bird catcher is coming. You should fly away quickly!" The male peacock said, "My tail is wet from the rain. Now I can't fly, otherwise my beautiful tail will be damaged, and I will not

emerald
adj. 翡翠的, 祖母绿的

superior
adj. 优越的

be beautiful."

In a short time, the bird catcher arrived and the male peacock, which cherished its tail, was caught.

Moral

The fable warns people not to attach too much importance to their own advantages; otherwise these advantages will become the burden and even lead to the disaster of killing themselves.

良狗捕鼠

《吕氏春秋》

　　古时候,齐国有一个善于识狗的人,他能一眼看出狗的优劣。他的邻居委托他找一只能捕捉老鼠的狗。齐人非常用心认真,用了一年的时间,终于找到了一条好狗,并且亲自将好狗送到邻居家里。邻居非常感谢。

　　一晃数年过去了,邻居家的老鼠没有一点减少的迹象,甚至比以前更严重了。那只狗呢?长得更健壮了,浑身是劲,就是没有看见它捕过一只老鼠。邻居气鼓鼓地找到齐人,质问他为什么这条好狗不捕老鼠。齐人明白了邻居的来意,忍不住哈哈大笑:"这确实是只好狗,但它的志向在于捕捉獐、麋、猪、鹿这类野兽,而不是老鼠。想让它捉老鼠的话,就捆绑住它的后腿。"后来,这个邻居绑住了狗的后腿,这狗才捉老鼠。

【寓意】有了人才如果不知善用,就无法发挥他们的作用。要创造条件,人尽其才,物尽其用。

Good Dog Catching Rats

From *Master Lü's Spring and Autumn Annals*

In ancient times, a man of Qi State was good at recognizing dogs, and could tell at a glance whether they were good or bad. His neighbor commissioned him to find a dog that could catch rats. Carefully and earnestly, the man spent a year finding a good dog and delivered it to the neighbor's house in person. The neighbor was very grateful.

Several years later, the neighbor's rat problem showed no sign of **abating**, and was even worse than before. And the dog? It grew stronger and stronger, and was never seen to catch any rats. The neighbor angrily found the man of Qi State, asking him why the dog did not catch any rats. The man understood the neighbor's purpose and couldn't help laughing, "It is indeed a good dog, but it has the ambition to catch **roes**, elks, pigs, deer and other wild beasts, rather than rats. If you want the dog to catch rats, just tie its hind legs." Later, the neighbor tied the dog's hind legs, so that the dog began to catch rats.

abate

v. 减弱，减少

roe

n. 獐

❋ Moral

If we don't know how to make good use of the talented persons we own, we won't be able to discover their role. It is necessary to create the conditions for making full use of talents as well as the resources.

两小儿辩日

《列子》

一天,孔子向东游历,看到两个小孩在争论不休。一个小孩说:"我认为太阳刚刚升起时离我们近一些,中午的时候远一些。"另一个小孩说:"我认为太阳刚刚升起时离我们远一些,而中午时近一些。"

孔子问:"你们这样说有什么理由呢?"

一个小孩说:"太阳刚出来时像车盖一样大,到了中午却像个盘子,这不是因为远时看起来小而近时看起来大吗?"

另一个小孩说:"太阳刚出来时有清凉的感觉,到了中午却像把手伸进热水里一样,这不是因为近时热而远时凉吗?"

两个小孩说得都有道理,孔子也无法判断谁是谁非。

两个小孩笑着说:"像您这样的大学问家,也有不知道的啊!"

【寓意】太阳远近的问题,是一个科学问题,需要科学求证,在孔子那个时代还不能回答这个问题。寓言故事揭示了两点:一是知识是无穷的,宇宙无限、学无止境;二是孔子实事求是,敢于承认自己学识不足。

Two Kids Arguing about the Sun

From *Liezi*

One day, Confucius went east to publicize his theories when he met two kids arguing about the sun. One said, "I think the sun is closer to us when it just rises in the morning and farther away from us at noon." The other argued, "I think the sun is farther away from us when it just rises and closer to us at noon."

Confucius asked, "What reasons do you have for saying so?"

One child replied, "When the sun comes out, it is as big as a cart **canopy**, but it at noon looks like a plate. Isn't it because it looks small when far away and big when near?"

canopy
n. 罩篷，罩盖

The other child argued, "When the sun comes out in the morning, it feels cool and **refreshing**, but at noon it is hot like putting your hands into hot water. Isn't it because it is hot in the near place and cool in the far?"

refresh
v. 使凉爽

Both kids had a point, and even Confucius could not judge who was right and who was wrong.

The two kids laughed and said, "For a great scholar like you, there still are things beyond your knowledge!"

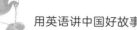

◆ Moral

The distance of the sun is a scientific question, requiring scientific **verification**, which could not be answered in the era of Confucius. The fable reveals two points: First, knowledge is infinite, the universe is infinite, and there is no limit to learning; second, Confucius was realistic, and dared to admit his own lack of knowledge.

verification
n. 证实，验证

买椟还珠

《韩非子》

楚国有个人到郑国去卖珠宝。为了能卖个好价钱,他用上等的木材给珠宝做了一个非常精致的盒子,并且请技艺高超的雕刻师在盒子的外面刻上各种各样美丽的花纹,又用名贵的香料把盒子薰得芳香扑鼻,并且还在盒子上面点缀上许多珠玉,用玫瑰色和翠绿色的宝石装饰起来。

珠宝商带着他精心准备的珠宝去了郑国。果真不出所料,展出没多久,很多郑国人都聚拢过来,对他盛放珠宝的盒子赞不绝口,对盒子里的珠宝却视而不见。商人紧张起来,毕竟他要卖的是珠宝。

这时,有个郑国人,出高价买了他的珠宝。可是他刚走了几步,却又折了回来。珠宝商以为他改变了主意,想退掉珠宝。谁知那人走到珠宝商面前,小心翼翼地打开盒子,取出里面的珠宝递给珠宝商说:"刚才走得匆忙,竟然没发现盒子里有颗珠宝。这肯定是先生您放到里面去的,我是专程来归还珠宝的。"

珠宝商拿着郑国人还回来的珠宝,惊讶得合不拢嘴。

【寓意】一个素养不高、缺乏鉴别能力的人,往往会丢掉真正宝贵的东西,而把那些价值并不高的东西当成宝贝。

Buying the Casket Without the Pearl

From *Hanfeizi*

A man of Chu State went to Zheng State to sell a pearl. In order to sell it at a good price, he made a very **delicate** case for the pearl out of fine wood, asked a skilled **sculptor** to carve all kinds of beautiful patterns on the outside of the box, perfumed it with precious spices, and mounted it with white jades, adorned it with rose-colored stone and sewed green jadeite onto its fringes.

delicate *adj.* 精致的

sculptor *n.* 雕刻家

The jeweler went to Zheng State with the jewelry he had carefully prepared. As expected, not long after the exhibition, many people of Zheng State gathered around and praised the case in which it contained the pearl, but turned a blind eye to the pearl in it. The merchant became nervous, for after all what he wanted to sell was the pearl.

At that moment, a man of Zheng paid a high price for his jewelry. However, after just taking a few steps, he went back. The jeweler thought that the man had changed his mind and wanted to return the jewelry. But the man walked up to the jeweler, carefully opened the wooden case, took out the pearl inside and handed it to the jeweler, saying, "I walked in a hurry just now, so I didn't notice that there was a pearl in the case. It must have been put in by you, sir. I came all the way here to return it."

The jeweler took the pearl returned by the man of Zheng, being **astonished** and unable to keep his mouth shut.

astonished
adj. 吃惊的，感到十分惊讶的

❖ Moral

A poorly educated person, lacking in a good judgement, tends to throw away what is really valuable and treat as treasure what is not of high value.

卖弄小聪明的猎人

《柳河东集》

据说,鹿怕山狸,山狸怕老虎,老虎怕马熊。

楚国有个猎人,打猎的本领不强,但他会耍小聪明。他用竹管削成口哨,能逼真地模仿各种野兽的叫声。他常学羊叫、鹿鸣,把黄羊、梅花鹿引到跟前捕杀。

有一次,他又带着弓箭、火药等工具上山了。他用口哨吹出鹿鸣的声音。没想到,逼真的鹿鸣声把想吃鹿肉的山狸引出来了。猎人吓了一跳,连忙吹出老虎的吼叫声,把山狸吓跑了。但逼真的虎吼又招来一只饿虎。猎人更慌了,急忙吹出马熊的吼声,把老虎吓跑了。他刚想喘一口气,一只张牙舞爪的马熊闻声寻来。这个只会耍小聪明的猎人再也吹不出别的野兽叫声来吓唬马熊了。他魂飞魄散,瘫成一团,听任马熊扑上来把他吃了。

【寓意】我们做任何事情都要凭真本事,靠踏踏实实的劳动,不能靠小聪明、靠蒙骗,否则,就会像这个猎人一样,聪明反被聪明误,落得个可悲的下场。

寓言故事

Hunter Playing Petty Tricks

From *Anthology of Liu Hedong*

It is said that deer are afraid of beavers, beavers afraid of tigers, and tigers afraid of brown bears.

There was a hunter in Chu State, who was not very good at hunting but could play **petty tricks**. He cut a bamboo pipe into a whistle, and could realistically imitate the cries of various wild animals. He often **imitated** cries of sheep and deer, and attracted Mongolian gazelle and sika deer so as to hunt and kill them.

He once went up the mountain with bows, arrows, gunpowder and other things. He used the whistle to make a sound of deer crying. Unexpectedly, the vivid cry of deer drew out some beavers who wanted to eat them. The hunter got frightened and hurriedly made the roar of tigers, which scared away the beavers. However, the vivid roar of tigers attracted a hungry tiger. The hunter panicked even more, and **hastily** made the roar of brown bears, which scared away the tiger. As he tried to catch his breath, a brown bear, baring its fangs and brandishing its claws, heard the sound and came to him. The hunter with only petty tricks could not make any more noises of other animals so as to scare away the brown bear. He was out of his mind and collapsed onto the ground, leaving the bear to jump on him

petty tricks
小聪明

imitate
v. 模仿

hastily
adv. 急速地，仓促地

and eat him.

❋ Moral

We must do everything on the basis of real ability and down-to-earth work, rather than petty tricks or deception. Otherwise, we will end up like the hunter, who was wronged by petty tricks and ended up in a **miserable** situation.

miserable
adv. 可怜的

寓言故事

猫头鹰搬家

《说苑》

猫头鹰遇到斑鸠,斑鸠问:"猫头鹰老兄,你要去哪儿啊?"

"我准备搬到东乡去。"

"为什么呢?"

"西乡的人都讨厌我的叫声,我实在住不下去了。"

"老兄,依我说,关键是你得把叫声调整得悦耳一点,或者干脆夜里就别叫了;要不,别说搬到东乡,搬到哪儿也招人讨厌!"

猫头鹰停下脚步,认真思考着斑鸠的忠告。

【寓意】别人对自己有意见,要从自身找原因,不要埋怨环境,甚至回避问题。应该正视自己的不足,克服自己的缺点,从而改变大家的看法。

An Owl Moving Its Nest

From *The Garden of Anecdotes*

Once an owl met a turtledove, and the turtledove asked, "Brother Owl, where are you going?"

"I'm going to move to the East Village."

"Why?"

"Everyone in the West Village hates my screams, and I can't **afford** to live there anymore."

afford

v. 买得起，承担得起

"Brother Owl, I think the key is that you need to make your screaming a little more pleasant, or simply stop screaming at night. Otherwise, let alone in the East Village, it's annoying everywhere you move!"

The owl stopped and seriously considered the advice from the turtledove.

Moral

When other people have opinions about us, we should not **blame** the environment or even avoid the problem, but look for the cause in ourselves. We should face up to our own shortcomings and overcome them, so as to change other people's opinions.

blame

v. 抱怨

寓言故事

明年再改

《孟子》

有个人专门偷邻居家的鸡,一天偷一只,不偷就手心发痒。

别人劝告他:"这样做太不道德了。再偷下去,不会有好下场的,赶快改了吧。"

这个偷鸡贼也想洗手不干了,但是下不来决心,他对劝告的人说:"好吧,我听您的。但是,我的偷瘾太大了,要我马上歇手,我办不到。这样吧,以前我每天偷一只鸡,从明天开始,改为每月偷一只鸡,到明年就可以彻底不偷了。"

如果已经知道这样做不对,那就赶快停止好了,为什么还要等到明年呢?

【寓意】知错就要下决心立即改正,不能找借口拖延时间,更不能明知故犯!

用英语讲中国好故事

Stop Stealing Next Year

From *Mencius*

There was a man who specialized in stealing his neighbors' chickens. The man developed the habit of stealing one every day, and his palms would get itchy if he didn't steal. He was advised, "It is so **immoral**. If you keep stealing, you won't have a good ending, so get rid of your bad habit."

immoral
adj. 不道德

The thief also wanted to quit, but he couldn't make up his mind. Thus, he said to those who advised him, "All right, I'll listen to you. However, my addiction to stealing is so great that it is impossible for me to stop right away. Well, I used to steal one chicken every day, but from tomorrow I'll switch to stealing one chicken every month, so that I'll completely call an end to stealing by next year."

If we already know it's not right, then just stop it as soon as possible. Why wait until next year?

Moral

If we know there is something wrong with us, we must make up our mind to correct it immediately, rather than find an excuse to **procrastinate**, let alone commit a willful offence!

procrastinate
v. 拖延，耽搁

其父善游

《吕氏春秋》

有个等着过江的人,看见一个大人正拉着一个小孩,要把他投到江里去。小孩子哭喊着,拼命挣扎。

过江人问:"这么小的孩子,你把他扔到江里,不就淹死了吗?"

那个大人说:"不会。"

"怎么不会呢?江水那么深。"过江人疑惑地问。

大人说:"他父亲是个游泳高手。"

就算父亲擅长游泳,难道儿子就擅长游泳吗?

【寓意】父亲会游泳和儿子有一点关系吗?本领技能是后天勤奋努力学习的结果,它不遗传。寓言中那个大人的荒唐思维,我们身边不是也有吗?

The Son of a Good Swimmer

From *Master Lü's Spring and Autumn Annals*

A man, waiting to cross the river, saw an adult pulling a child and trying to throw him into the river. The child cried out and struggled desperately.

The man waiting to cross the river asked, "For such a little child, will he be **drowned** when you throw him into the river?"

drown
v. 溺死

The adult said, "No."

"Why won't he? The river is so deep." the man asked doubtfully.

The adult answered, "His father is a good swimmer."

Even if his father is good at swimming, does it mean the son will also be good at swimming?

Moral

Does the father's ability to swim have anything to do with his son's? Skills are the result of hard work and effort, which cannot be inherited. Don't you think people around us sometimes also have the same absurd thought as the adult in the fable?

寓言故事

齐人偷金

《吕氏春秋》

　　从前，有个齐国人，成天想得到金子。他白天想的是金子，夜里梦的是金子。

　　有一天，他早早起床，穿好衣服，赶到集市上，走进一家金店，从柜子里抓起一块金子就跑。当场就被店主抓住了，扭送官府。

　　官员审问他："光天化日之下，当着那么多人的面，你都敢拿人家的金子，胆子不小啊！"

　　齐国人回答："我眼里只有金子，根本没有看到人。"

【寓意】利欲熏心才会目中无人，这则寓言形容人因贪利而失去了理智，做出令人不齿的事情。

A Man of Qi Stealing Gold

From *Master Lü's Spring and Autumn Annals*

Once upon a time, there was a man of Qi State, who wanted gold all day long. He thought of gold during the day and dreamed of gold at night.

One day he got up very early, put on his clothes, rushed to the market, walked into a gold shop, grabbed a piece of gold from the cabinet and ran away. On the spot the shopkeeper caught him and sent him to the government.

The official **interrogated** him, "In broad daylight, in front of so many people, you stole other people's gold. How dare you!"

interrogate
v. 审问，讯问

The man replied, "I only see gold in my eyes, and no people at all."

❖ Moral

Being blinded by greed, a person cares for nobody. The fable describes the person who has lost his mind and done something disgraceful because of his greed for profit.

寓言故事

千金买马首

《战国策》

战国时期,燕国曾经被齐国打败。燕昭王即位后,想振兴国家,向郭隗请教救国方法。郭隗给燕王讲了下面这个故事:

古代有个国君,愿意出一千金来购买一匹千里马,但三年都没有买到。这桩事成了国君最大的心病。这时,有个人自告奋勇,替国君去寻找千里马。国君非常高兴,让这人带了一千金,立即出发。

这人用了三个月时间,终于打听到某地有一匹千里马。他立即赶到那儿,可惜,这匹千里马已经病死了。怎么办?这人考虑再三,决定用五百金买下这匹死马的头,带回来献给国君。

国君见是一颗死马的脑袋,勃然大怒,说:"你怎么把死马买回来了,而且还用了五百金呢?"

这人连忙回答:"请君王息怒。千里马非常难求,没有十分的虔诚,马主人是不肯轻易出手的。现在君王您连死去的千里马,都肯用五百金买下来,何况活马呢?消息传出去,大家肯定认为您是真心买马,很快就会有人把千里马送到君王面前。"果然,不到一年时间,各地就送来了三匹千里马。

郭隗讲完这个故事,便请燕王重用自己。他对燕王说:"天下贤士看到像我这样才疏学浅的人尚且得到您的尊重,就会知道水平比我高的能人,当然更会得到您加倍的尊敬和重用,天下人才就会不远千里来投奔您了。"

【寓意】招聘人才,不仅要有诚心,还要讲究方法,以实际行动赢得人才的心。

Buying Head of Horse with Gold

From *Stratagems of the Warring States*

During the Warring States Period, Yan State was once defeated by Qi State. After King Zhao of Yan State ascended the throne, he wanted to revive his kingdom and asked Guo Wei for advice on how to save the nation. Guo Wei told the King the following story:

In ancient times, there was a King who was willing to pay one thousand taels of gold for a swift horse, which could run a thousand *li* within a day. The King had been looking for the horse for three years but all in vain. It became the King's biggest worry. Then, a man **volunteered** to go in search of a swift horse on behalf of the King. The King was so pleased that he asked the man to take one thousand taels of gold and set out immediately.

It took the man three months to find out that there was a swift horse somewhere. He rushed there at once. Unfortunately, the horse had been sick and died already. What was to be done? The man thought it over, and decided to buy the head of the dead horse with five hundred taels of gold and brought it back to the King.

Seeing that it was a dead horse's head, the King flew into a rage and said, "How did you buy the dead horse back even with five hundred taels of gold?"

volunteer

v. 自告奋勇

The man hurriedly replied, "Please calm down, Your Majesty. It is very difficult to get the swift horses, and the owner of the horses will not easily sell them if the buyer has no great **sincerity**. Now, Your Majesty, you are even willing to buy the dead horse with five hundred taels of gold, let alone a live one. When the word spreads, everyone will believe in your determination to buy swift horses, and soon someone will send a horse to the palace." Sure enough, in less than a year, three swift horses were sent from all over the state.

After Guo Wei finished the story, he asked the King of Yan to put himself in a key position. He said, "If the wise men in the world see that a man like me with little knowledge and talent is still respected by you, they will know that those with a higher level than me will certainly be doubly respected and used by you. Then the talents will come all the way from thousands of miles away to join you."

sincerity

n. 诚意，真挚

❖ Moral

To recruit talents, we should not only be sincere, but also pay attention to methods, and we can win the hearts of talents with practical actions and measures.

穷和尚和富和尚

《白鹤堂诗文集》

四川的边远地区有两个和尚,一个穷,一个富。

有一天,穷和尚对富和尚说:"我想到佛教圣地南海去朝拜,你说行不行?"

富和尚问:"来回好几千里地,你靠什么去呢?"

穷和尚说:"我只要一个喝水的瓶子,一个吃饭的泥盆就行了。"

富和尚听了哈哈大笑,说:"几年前,我就下决心要租条船到南海去朝圣,但是,凭我的条件,到现在还没能办到。你靠一只破瓶子,一个泥瓦盆就要到南海去?真是白日做梦!"

一年以后,富和尚还在为租船筹钱,穷和尚却已经从南海朝圣回来了。

【寓意】富和尚和穷和尚代表两种生活态度。富和尚"常立志",立在口头上;穷和尚说到做到,就能办成事。

寓言故事

Two Monks

From *Collected Poems by Peng Duanshu*

In a remote area of Sichuan there were two monks, one poor and one rich.

One day, the poor monk said to the rich monk, "I want to make a **pilgrimage** to the Nanhai Sea, a holy place of Buddhism. What do you think of it?"

pilgrimage
n. 朝圣

The rich monk asked, "It's thousands of miles for a round trip, and what do you rely on to get there?"

The poor monk replied, "All I need is a bottle to drink water from and a clay pot to eat from."

Hearing the words, the rich monk laughed and said, "A few years ago, I made up my mind to rent a boat to go on a pilgrimage to the Nanhai Sea. However, on my own terms, I have not been able to do so until nowadays. Do you want to go to the Nanhai Sea by relying on one broken bottle and one clay pot? What a daydream!"

A year later, the rich monk was still raising money for the lease of a boat, but the poor monk had already returned from his pilgrimage to the Nanhai Sea.

✤ Moral

The rich monk and the poor monk represent the two attitudes towards life. The rich monk "always make up his mind" and he cannot get things done only with his words; however, the poor monk always does what he says, and he can get things done with his actions.

寓言故事

人贵有自知之明

《战国策》

邹忌身高八尺,仪表堂堂,是齐国有名的帅哥。

一天早晨,邹忌穿戴好衣帽,照着镜子问妻子:"我和城北的徐先生比,谁更帅呢?"他的妻子说:"您最帅,徐先生怎么能比得上您呢?"城北的徐先生据说是齐国的美男子。邹忌不相信自己比徐先生帅,于是又问他的妾:"我和徐先生相比,谁更帅呢?"妾说:"徐先生哪能比得上您呢?"

有位客人来访,谈笑之余,邹忌想起昨天的事,就拿同样的问题问客人:"您看我和城北的徐先生哪个更帅呢?"客人毫不犹豫地说:"徐先生比不上您,您更帅。"

邹忌做了三次调查,结论都是一致的。但他并没有沾沾自喜,认为自己就是齐国最帅的人。恰巧有一天,城北的徐先生来拜访邹忌,邹忌仔细地看着他,自叹不如;再照镜子看看自己,更是觉得自己与徐先生相差甚远。

晚上躺在床上,邹忌反复思考这件事,终于想明白了一个道理:原来我身边的人都在恭维我。妻子说我帅,是因为偏爱我;妾说我帅,是因为害怕我;客人说我帅,是因为有求于我。看来,我是受了身边人的恭维而认不清自我了。

【寓意】人贵有自知之明。我们应该对自己有个清醒的认识,才不受身边人的蒙蔽。身边人之所以投其所好,是因为你的权势。

用英语讲中国好故事

The Significance of Self-knowledge

From *Stratagems of the Warring States*

Zou Ji, with an eight-*chi* height and an attractive appearance, was a famous handsome guy in Qi State.

One morning, Zou Ji put on his clothes and hat, looked in the mirror and asked his wife, "Who is more handsome, Mr. Xu in the north of the city or me?" His wife replied, "You are the most handsome. How can Mr. Xu compare with you?" However, Mr. Xu was said to be a very handsome guy in Qi State. Zou Ji did not believe that he was more handsome than Mr. Xu, so he asked his **concubine** the same question. The concubine replied the same way, "How can Mr. Xu compare with you?"

The next day, a guest came to visit. While talking and laughing, Zou Ji remembered what had happened yesterday and asked the guest the same question, "Which one of us do you think is more handsome, Mr. Xu in the north of the city or me?" The guest said without hesitation, "Mr. Xu is not as attractive as you, and you are more handsome."

Zou Ji made three investigations and all the answers were **unanimous**. However, he was not complacent and did not think he was the most handsome person in Qi State. One day, Zou Ji was coincidentally visited by Mr. Xu in the north of the city, and he carefully looked at Mr. Xu and

concubine
n. 妾

unanimous
adj. 一致的，一致同意的

sighed that he himself was **inferior**. Looking at himself in the mirror again, Zou Ji felt that he was far from Mr. Xu.

Lying in bed at night, Zou Ji pondered the matter over and over again, and finally figured out a truth: It turned out that all the people around me were flattering me. My wife said I was more handsome because she **was partial to** me; my concubine said I was more handsome because she was afraid of me; my guest said so because he wanted something from me. It seems that I have been so flattered by the people around me that I cannot recognize myself clearly.

❖ Moral

It is significant for people to have self-knowledge. We should keep a clear mind about ourselves, so as not to be deceived by those around us. Those around us take our fancy just because of our power.

inferior
adj. 比不上，较差的

be partial to sb.
偏爱某人

桑中生李

《六朝志怪小说选》

南顿有个叫张助的人，在田里种庄稼时发现一颗李子的核，本想拿走，回头看见空心的桑洞里有泥土，就把李核种在那里，并浇了一些水。

后来，有人看见桑树中又长出李树来，对此感到十分惊奇，就互相传说开来。有个患眼痛病的人在李树荫下休息，说："李树你让我的眼睛痊愈吧，我用小猪道谢。"眼痛这种小病，不久就会自行治愈。众人遂传闻李树是颗"神树"，能让瞎了的人重新看见，因此远近的人听到这消息都很激动，那树下常有数千辆马车，载着丰盛的酒肉。

时隔一年，张助出远门回来，看见这景象十分惊诧，说："这有什么神奇的？这就是我种的一棵李树罢了。"

【寓意】万事有源，遇见非同一般的现象，不要盲从轻信，要以冷静的头脑仔细分析推测，做出科学的解释。

寓言故事

Plum Growing out of Mulberry

From *Selected Stories of the Six Dynasties*

There was a man named Zhang Zhu in Nandun, who found a plum kernel while planting crops in his field and wanted to take it away. However, when he saw some soil in a hollow mulberry hole, he planted the plum kernel there and watered it.

Later, some people were amazed to see a plum tree growing out of the mulberry tree, and told others. A man suffering from eye pain rested under the shade of the plum tree and said, "Plum tree, please let my eyes heal, and I will thank you with a little pig." Such a minor illness as eye pain would be cured soon by itself. It was **rumored** that the plum tree was a "sacred tree" able to make the blind people see again, so people near and far heard the news and got very excited. There were often thousands of carriages together with sumptuous wine and meat under the tree.

One year later, Zhang Zhu returned from a long trip and was very surprised at what he saw, saying, "What's so amazing about this? This is just a plum tree I planted in a hollow mulberry hole."

rumor

v. 谣传

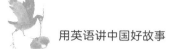

❖ Moral

Everything has its source. Thus, when we encounter unusual phenomena, we should not blindly follow and easily believe, but carefully analyze and **conjecture** with a calm mind, and finally make scientific explanation.

conjecture
v. 猜测

寓言故事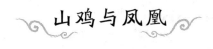

山鸡与凤凰

《笑林》

从前，有一个楚国人外出时在路上碰到一个挑着山鸡的村夫。因为这人没有见过山鸡，所以一见到长着漂亮羽毛和修长尾巴的山鸡就认定它不是一个俗物。他好奇地问村夫："你挑的是一只什么鸟？"那村夫见他不认识山鸡，便信口说道："是凤凰。"这楚人听了心中大喜，并感慨地说道："我以前只是听说有凤凰，今天终于见到了凤凰！你能不能把它卖给我？"村夫说："可以。"楚人出价十金。那村夫想："既然这个傻子把它当成了凤凰，我岂能只卖十金？"于是，村夫将卖价提高一倍，把山鸡卖掉了。

楚人高高兴兴地把山鸡带回家，打算第二天去给楚王献"凤凰"，可是谁知过了一夜山鸡就死了。这人望着僵硬的山鸡，顿时感到眼前一片灰暗。此刻他脑海里没有一丝吝惜金钱的想法，但对于不能将这种吉祥神物献给楚王却心痛不已。

这件事一传十，十传百，很快被楚王知道了。虽然楚王没有得到凤凰，但是被这个人有心献凤凰的忠心所感动。楚王派人把这个欲献凤凰的楚人召到宫中，赐给他比买山鸡多十倍的金子。

【寓意】善有善报，楚人虽然被骗，但他对楚王的忠心难能可贵，最终得到了回报。

Pheasant and Phoenix

From *Xiaolin*

Once upon a time, a man of Chu State met a villager carrying a pheasant on his way out. Since the man had never seen a pheasant before, he decided that the pheasant with beautiful feathers and a long tail was not a commonplace bird. Curiously, he asked the villager, "What kind of bird are you carrying?" The villager saw that the man did not know the pheasant, so he said at random, "It is a phoenix." The man said with great joy, "I had only heard of a phoenix before, but today I finally saw one! Can you sell it to me?" The villager replied, "Sure." The man of Chu offered ten taels of gold. The villager thought, "Since the fool man thinks of it as a phoenix, how can I sell it for only ten taels of gold?" Therefore, the villagers doubled the selling price, and sold the pheasant to the man of Chu.

The man brought the pheasant home happily, intending to offer it to the King of Chu the next day, but the pheasant died overnight. The man looked at the **stiff** pheasant and felt a sense of gloom. At the moment he had not a stingy thought about money in his mind, but a sad idea that he could not offer the pheasant to the King.

The story rapidly spread like wildfire, and the King of Chu soon heard about it. Although the King did not get the

stiff

adj. 僵硬的

phoenix, he was touched by the man who had the intention to offer it. The King of Chu sent one of his officials to summon the man to the palace and gave him gold, which was ten times more than the money he spent on the pheasant.

❖ Moral

The man was deceived, but his loyalty to the King of Chu was **invaluable** and was rewarded eventually.

invaluable
adj. 极为珍贵的，无价的

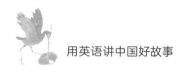

生木造屋

《吕氏春秋》

　　宋国大夫高阳应想盖一座宅院,就砍伐了很多木材做准备。等木材备齐了,他就找来工匠,催其即日动工建房。

　　工匠一看,新砍的木料连枝杈还没有削掉,树皮也没有刮掉。在树皮脱落的地方,露出光泽、湿润的白皙木芯。用这种木料怎么能马上盖房呢?所以工匠对高阳应说:"目前还不能开工。这些刚砍下来的木料含水太多、质地柔韧,抹泥承重以后容易变弯。初看起来,用这种木料盖的房子与用干木料盖的房子相比,差别不大,但是时间一长,用湿木料盖的房子容易倒塌。"

　　高阳应听了工匠的话,不以为然,反问道:"依你所见,不就是湿木料承重以后容易弯曲吗?你想过没有,湿木料干了也会变硬,稀泥巴干了也会变轻。你按我说的做就是了。"工匠只好遵照高阳应的吩咐去办。

　　不久,一幢新屋就落成了。可时间一长,新屋越来越往一边倾斜,高阳应怕出事故,只好搬出了新屋。没过多久,这幢房子果然倒塌了。

【寓意】我们做任何事情,都必须尊重实践经验和客观规律,而不能主观蛮干。否则,只会受到客观规律的惩罚。

寓言故事

Mansion Made of Raw Wood

From *Master Lü's Spring and Autumn Annals*

Gao Yangying, a senior official of Song State, wanted to build a mansion, so he cut down a lot of trees for preparation. When the lumber got ready, he called in a craftsman and **urged** him to start on the same day.

At first look, the craftsman found that even the branches of the newly-cut wood had not yet been cut off, nor had the bark of the wood been scraped off. In the place where some bark had fallen off, the **lustrous**, moist, fair and clear wooden core was exposed. How could a house be built immediately with this kind of wood? Thus the craftsman said to Gao Yangying, "We can't start the work now. The newly-cut wood contains too much water and is **pliable**, so it will bend easily after it is loaded with mud and made heavy. At first glance, there is not much difference between a house built with this sort of wet wood and the one built with that sort of dry wood, but the house built with wet wood is likely to collapse."

On hearing the craftsman's words, Gao Yangying disapproved and asked rhetorically, "In your opinion, wet wood is prone to bending after bearing weight. Have you ever thought that wet wood will be hard when it dries, and wet mud will be light when it dries? Just do what I

urge
v. 催促

lustrous
adj. 柔软光亮的

pliable
adj. 易弯曲的, 柔韧的

129

tell you." The craftsman had to follow Gao Yangying's instructions.

Soon after, the new mansion was completed. However, as time passed the mansion leaned more and more to one side, and Gao Yangying had no choice but to move out of it being afraid of an accident. It was before long that the mansion really collapsed.

Moral

We must not be subjective and **foolhardy**, but respect practical experience and objective laws in everything we do. Otherwise, we will only be punished by them.

foolhardy
adj. 有勇无谋的，莽撞的

寓言故事

宋人疑盗

《韩非子》

从前，宋国有个富翁。有一天，一场大暴雨把他家的土围墙冲塌了一段。雨停后，他儿子说："父亲，快找个泥瓦匠来修墙吧，要不会有小偷进来偷东西。"住在隔壁的一位老人也劝富翁："你得赶快把冲塌的墙修补好，现在盗贼多，围墙缺了不安全。"

没想到，当天夜里小偷就从缺口进来，偷走了好多值钱的东西。

事后，富翁见人就夸自己的儿子有远见，料事如神，而对提出同样忠告的邻居十分怀疑，认为东西可能就是隔壁的那个老人偷的。

【寓意】同一个建议，从儿子嘴里说出来的是忠告，从邻居嘴里说出来就成了猜疑的依据。这完全是凭着关系远近做出的主观判断。我们办任何事情绝不能凭主观臆测和个人感情，一定要注意调查研究，尊重客观事实。

A Man of Song Suspicious of Stealing

From *Hanfeizi*

Once upon a time, there was a rich man in Song State. One day, a heavy rainstorm **washed down** a section of the earthen fence of his house. When the rain stopped, his son said, "Father, find a bricklayer to repair the earthen wall so that thieves won't come in and steal thing." An old man who lived next door also advised the rich man, "You have to repair the collapsed wall as soon as possible. Now there are many thieves and it is not safe to have one section of the fence missing."

Unexpectedly, a thief came in through the gap that night and stole a lot of valuable things.

Afterwards, the rich man praised his son for being far-sighted and **predictable**, while he was very suspicious of the neighbor who gave the same advice, thinking that the things might have been stolen by the old man next door.

wash down
冲倒

predictable
adj. 有预见的

Moral

As for the same piece of advice, what came out of the son is advice, but what came out of the neighbor became the basis for suspicion. It is entirely a subjective judgment based on the **proximity** of personal relationship. We must never do anything based on subjective assumptions or personal feelings, but always pay attention to investigation and respect objective facts.

proximity
n.(时间、空间或关系)
接近,邻近

束氏蓄猫

《龙门子凝道记》

卫国有个姓束的人，没有别的嗜好，专爱养猫。他家养了一百多只大大小小、颜色不同的猫。这些猫先把自己家的老鼠捉光了，后来又把周围邻居家的老鼠捉光了。猫没吃的，饿得喵喵直叫。束氏就每天到菜场买肉喂猫。

几年过去了，老猫生小猫，小猫又生小猫。这些后生的猫，由于每天吃惯了现成的肉，饿了就叫，一叫就有肉吃，吃饱了就晒太阳，睡懒觉，竟不知道世界上还有老鼠，也忘了自己负有捕鼠的天职。

城南有户人家老鼠成灾。他们听说束家猫多，就借了一只猫回家逮老鼠。束家的猫看见地上那些乱窜的老鼠耸着两只小耳朵，瞪着两只小眼睛，翘着两撇小胡须，一个劲儿地吱吱乱叫，感到非常新鲜，又有点害怕，只是蹲在桌子上看，不敢跳下去捉。这家的主人看见猫这么不中用，气坏了，使劲把猫推了下去。猫害怕极了，吓得直叫。老鼠一见它那副傻样，估计没有多大能耐，就一拥而上，有的啃猫脚爪，有的咬猫尾巴。猫又怕又疼，使劲一跳，逃跑了。

【寓意】这则寓言启示长期养尊处优、缺乏锻炼的生活会导致人生存能力下降，甚至丧失的道理。

用英语讲中国好故事

Shu Raising Cats

From *Allegories Collected by Song Lian*

There was a man surnamed Shu in Wei State, who had no other hobbies but to raise cats. He had more than one hundred cats of different sizes and colors, which caught all the rats in his own house firstly, and then all the rats in the **neighborhood**. At last the cats had nothing to eat and meowed with hunger. Shu went to the market every day to buy meat to feed the cats.

Several years later, the adult cats gave birth to kittens, and the kittens gave birth to cat litters after growing up. These cats, born in the following years, were used to eating ready-made meat every day. When they were hungry, they would call out for food, and when they were full, they would **sunbathe** and sleep lazily, not knowing that there were rats in the world, and forgetting that they had the duty to catch rats.

A family in the south of the same town **was infested with** rats. When they heard the Shu family had many cats, they borrowed one of the cats and brought it home to catch rats. When the cat saw the rats scrambling on the ground, erecting their small ears, staring with their small eyes and tilting their small beards, **squeaking** and squeaking again, it felt very fresh and a little scared, and just **crouched** on

neighborhood
n. 邻里

sunbathe
v. 晒太阳

be infested with
多得成灾，被……充斥

squeak
v. 吱吱叫

crouch
v. 蹲下

the table and dared not jump down to catch them. The owner of the house was so angry when he saw the cat was so useless that he pushed it down. The cat was so scared that it screamed with fear. As soon as the rats saw its silly appearance, they estimated that it was not very capable, so they swarmed on it, some gnawing at its paws and others biting its tail. The cat felt frightened and pained, jumped with all its might and escaped.

❀ Moral

The fable reveals that a prolonged life of **pampering** and lack of exercise can lead to a decline or even loss of survival abilities.

pamper

v. 细心照顾，娇惯

太阳的样子

《东坡全集》

从前有个人,生下来就双目失明。他每天感受到阳光的温暖,却不知道太阳的模样,便向看得见的人请教。有个人拿来一只铜盘,敲着让他听听,告诉他:"太阳的形状是圆的,就像这只铜盘。"盲人听到铛铛的响声,便连连点头:"喔,我知道了,我知道了。"

过了几天,盲人在街上听到铛铛的钟声,就高兴地喊道:"这是太阳!太阳出来了!"有人对他说:"错了,那不是太阳。太阳会发光,就像蜡烛一样。"边说边递给他一支蜡烛。盲人仔细地把蜡烛摸了一遍,连连点头说:"喔,这回我知道了,原来太阳是这样的。"

又过了几天,盲人随手摸到了一根短笛。他又高兴地喊了起来:"这该是太阳了吧!这该是太阳了吧!"

【寓意】寓言中的盲人闹了笑话,主要有两个原因:一是由于生理上的缺陷,盲人看不见;二是他把从别人那里获得的片面的间接经验误以为全面的认识,并且十分主观地做出了判断。学习别人的间接经验固然重要,但是一定要经过自己的亲身实践加以检验和完善,只有这样,才能有比较全面的认识,做出比较准确的判断。

Appearance of the Sun

From *Complete Works by Su Dongpo*

Once upon a time, a man was born blind. He felt the warmth of the sun every day and knew nothing about what the sun looked like, so he asked whoever could see. Someone else brought a brass plate and knocked on it for him to hear, telling him, "The sun is round in shape, just like this plate." After the blind man heard the **clanging** sound, he nodded his head, "Oh, I get it, I get it."

clang
v. 叮当作响

A few days later, the blind man heard the bell clanging in the street and shouted with joy, "It's the sun! The sun is coming out!" He was told, "Wrong. It's not the sun. The sun glows, just like a candle." After being told, he was handed a candle. The blind man touched the candle carefully and nodded his head, saying, "Oh, now I know that the sun is like this."

After a few more days, the blind man touched a flute at hand. He shouted again with joy, "It must be the sun! It must be the sun!"

❋ Moral

In the fable, the blind man made a joke for two main reasons: Firstly, the blind man could not see due to a physical defect; secondly, he mistook the one-sided indirect experience from others for the comprehensive understanding, and made a very subjective judgment. It is important for us to learn from others' indirect experience, but it must be tested and perfected through our own practice. Only in this way can we have a more comprehensive understanding and make a more accurate judgment.

螳螂捕蝉，黄雀在后

《说苑》

吴王准备进攻楚国，他告诉群臣："我决心已定，谁也别想阻止，否则决不轻饶！"大臣们虽然心里都知道吴国目前的实力还不够雄厚，应该养精蓄锐，但谁也不敢乱说话。

大臣中有位年轻人，下朝后心中仍然无法安宁。他觉得不能因为担心个人安危而不顾国家安危。他在自家花园里踱来踱去，目光无意中落到树上的一只蝉身上，立刻有了主意。

第二天一早，年轻人就来到王宫的后花园内，他知道吴王每天上朝前都会到这里散步。不一会儿，吴王果然来了，年轻人装着没有看见吴王，眼睛紧盯着一棵树，手里还擒着一只弹弓。吴王纳闷地问道："喂，在做什么呢？"年轻人急忙施礼赔罪道："刚才只顾看那树上的蝉和螳螂，竟不知大王到来，请您恕罪。"

吴王挥挥手，好奇地问："你看到什么了？"

年轻人说："我看到一只蝉在喝露水，丝毫没有觉察一只螳螂正弓着腰准备捕食它，而螳螂也想不到一只黄雀正瞄准了自己，黄雀更想不到我手中的弹弓会要它的命……"

听了这番话，吴王恍然大悟："我明白了。"

终于，吴王打消了攻打楚国的念头。

【寓意】考虑问题、处理事情时，要深思熟虑，居安思危，不能只顾眼前利益，而不考虑身后的祸患。

The Cicada, the Praying Mantis and the Sparrow

From *The Garden of Anecdotes*

The King of Wu State was preparing to attack Chu State, and he told his ministers, "I am determined. No one should try to stop me, or he will never be forgiven!" Although the ministers knew in their minds that Wu State was not strong enough at the moment and should build up strength and store up energy, none of them dared to speak out.

There was a young man among the ministers, who still could not find peace in his mind after leaving the court. He felt that he could not **disregard** the safety of the country because of himself. Pacing in his garden, he immediately got a good idea after his eyes fell on a cicada in a tree unwittingly.

The next morning, the young man went to the back garden of the palace, where he knew the King would take his daily walk before going to court. Soon, the King of Wu did come, and the young man pretended not to see him, staring intently at a tree and holding a **slingshot** in his hand. The King of Wu wondered, "Hey, what are you doing?" The young man hurriedly offered an apology, "I was just looking at a cicada on that tree and a praying

disregard
v. 不顾，忽视

slingshot
n. 弹弓

mantis behind it, so I didn't even know you were coming, Your Majesty, please forgive me."

The King waved his hand and asked curiously, "What did you see?"

The young man said, "I saw a cicada drinking dew, unaware that a praying mantis was bowing its waist to prey on the cicada, but the mantis could not have imagined that a goldfinch was aiming its beak at itself, nor could the goldfinch have imagined that the slingshot in my hand would kill it ..."

After hearing these words, it **dawned on** the King of Wu, "I see."

Finally, the King of Wu gave up the idea to attack Chu State.

dawn on

v. 认识到，明白

❖ Moral

When considering problems and dealing with matters, we should not just focus on immediate benefits without considering the disasters behind us, but be thoughtful and consider risks in times of peace.

五十步笑百步

《孟子》

战国时期,魏国国君梁惠王请教孟子:"我对国家那可真是够尽心的啦!河内收成不好,遭饥荒,我就把那里的百姓迁移到河东,把河东的粮食运到河内;河东遭了饥荒,我也如此办。我注意到邻国的君王没有像我这样用心的。可是,邻国的百姓并不因此而减少,我的百姓也没有因此而增多,这是为什么呢?"

孟子回答说:"大王喜欢打仗,那就让我用打仗作比喻吧。战场上只要战鼓响起,士兵就会拼死搏斗。打败的一方,就会丢盔弃甲,仓皇逃跑。有人跑了一百步,有人跑了五十步。如果逃跑五十步的人嘲笑一百步的,说他是贪生怕死的逃兵,您说可以吗?"

惠王说:"不可以。五十步和一百步,都是逃跑呀!"

孟子说:"大王既然明白这个道理,怎么能够希望自己的百姓比邻国的多呢?"

【寓意】看事情要看本质,不要被表面现象所迷惑。梁惠王尽管对百姓生活关心有加,但战争给百姓带来的伤害更大。

寓言故事

The Pot Calling the Kettle Black

From *Mencius*

During the Warring States Period, King Hui of Wei State, asked Mencius for advice, "I have spent a lot of time and effort on governing my country. When there were poor harvests and **famine** in Henei, north of the Yellow River, I **evacuated** the people there to Hedong, east of the Yellow River and moved the grain from Hedong to Henei. When there was a famine in Hedong, I would do the same way. As far as I could notice, none of the rulers of the neighboring states are diligent as I am. But the population of the neighboring states does not decrease, and the population of my state does not increase. Why is this so?"

"My lord likes fighting battles," Mencius replied, "so let me make an **analogy** with war. As soon as the drums of war sound in the battlefield, the soldiers would fight to the death. The defeated side would throw away their armor and run away in haste. Someone runs one hundred paces, someone runs fifty. What if the one who runs fifty paces mocks the one who runs one hundred paces and calls him a deserter greedy for life and afraid of death, do you think it's okay?"

The King replied, "No. The latter didn't go one hundred paces, but they did run away all the same."

famine
n. 饥荒

evacuate
v. 撤离，转移

analogy
n. 比喻

Mencius said, "My lord, since you understand it well, how can you hope that your people are more numerous than those of your neighbors?"

Moral

We'd better pay more attention to the **essence** rather than the phenomena. Superficially, King Hui of Wei took care of his people, but in essence he launched the war that brought more harm to his people.

essence

n. 实质，本质，精髓

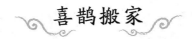

喜鹊搬家

《淮南子》

喜鹊很聪明，新年刚刚来临，它就预料到今年多风，特别是春秋季节，风会刮得异常猛烈。

它忙碌了好几天，终于把自己原来筑在树顶上的鹊窝搬到下面的枝丫上来了。

这一来，大风不可能把它的鹊窝吹落了。但是，别的灾难接踵而来，鹊窝离地面太近了，大人经过这里，伸手就把小喜鹊摸走了，小孩子经过这里，也用竹竿挑窝里的鹊蛋。

聪明的喜鹊只知道防备远难，却忘了防备近患。

【寓意】远难和近患都应该考虑到，否则就会顾此失彼。喜鹊的遭遇告诉我们，要学会全面地观察、分析和解决问题。

The Magpie's Nest

From *Huainanzi*

A magpie was very clever, and as soon as the New Year came it could predict that in the upcoming year there would be more wind and the wind would be extremely strong especially in the spring and autumn.

After being busy for several days, the magpie finally moved its nest to the branches below from the top of a tree.

As a result, the strong wind could not **blow off** the magpie's nest, but other disasters followed one by one. For examples, when adults passed by here they reached out to take little magpies away for the nest was too close to the ground; when children passed by here they took the eggs in the magpie's nest with a bamboo pole.

The smart magpie only knew how to **guard against** difficulties in the distance, but forgot to guard against troubles nearby.

blow off
吹掉

guard against
提防

Moral

We should **take into account** both difficulties in the distance and troubles nearby, otherwise we will attend one thing and lose sight of another. The magpie's bad experience tells us that we should learn to observe, analyze and solve problems in an all-round way.

take into account
考虑

心不在马

《韩非子》

古时候,晋国的王子期驾驭马车的技术高超,很多人都向他学习。

赵襄王也拜王子期为师学习驾车。刚学不久,掌握了基本技巧后,赵襄王就约王子期比赛,看谁驾车跑得快。赵襄王换了三次马,三次都输了。

赵襄王埋怨说:"你并没有把驾车的真本事教给我,还留了一手啊!"王子期听后,不慌不忙地回答:"大王您先不要生气,我把自己知道的都毫无保留地传授给您了,而且您也掌握得非常好。问题在于您的心没有用到马身上。"

"这话怎么讲?"赵襄王一时听糊涂了。

王子期说:"凡驾驭马车特别要注重的是,要使马套在车辕里很舒适,人的注意力要集中在马上,这样才可以加快速度到达目的地。大王您在落后时就一心想快点追上我,跑在前面时又怕被我赶上。其实驾车比赛这件事,不是跑在前面就是落在后面。而您不管是跑在前面还是落在后面,都总是把心思放在比赛的输赢上,还有什么心思去注意马呢?这就是您落后的原因了。"

赵襄王恍然大悟,不禁哈哈大笑,要求再与王子期加赛三场。

【寓意】做事要目标明确,全神贯注。如果不专心,太在意结果,心思都放到胜负上,反而不能成功。

No Attention to Horses

From *Hanfeizi*

In ancient times, Wang Ziqi of Jin State was so skilled at driving a carriage that many people come to learn from him.

The King Xiang of Zhao State learned to drive under the **tutelage** of Wang Ziqi. Before long, mastering the basic skills, the King invited his supervisor to a race, so as to find who could drive the carriage faster. The King changed horses three times, but lost all three times.

tutelage

n. 指导，辅导

The King complained, "You didn't teach me your real driving skills, and you kept something from me." When Wang Ziqi heard, he replied unhurriedly, "Don't be angry yet, Your Majesty. I have taught you all what I know without reservation, and you have mastered it very well. The problem is that your heart is not put into the horse."

"How do you say that?" the King was confused for a moment.

Wang Ziqi replied, "What one should pay special attention to while driving is to make the horse comfortable in the shaft of a carriage and his attention should be put to the horse so that one can speed up to reach the destination. However, you want to catch up with me when you are lagging behind, and you are afraid of being caught up by

me when you are running in front. In fact, in a driving race, you are either in front or behind. No matter whether you are driving in front or behind, your mind is always on winning or losing the race and what else do you have to pay to the horse? That's why you're **lagging behind**."

The King suddenly came to his senses, couldn't help laughing, and asked for three more matches with Wang Ziqi, his supervisor.

lag behind
落后

Moral

Do things with clear goals and full concentration. If we are not focused and became too concerned with the outcome of winning or losing, we will not succeed.

兄弟争雁

《应谐录》

有一对兄弟外出打猎,看见远处飞来一群大雁,两人就张弓搭箭准备射雁。

哥哥说:"现在的雁肥,射下来煮着吃。"

弟弟反对说:"大鹅煮着吃好,大雁还是烤了吃,又香又酥。"

"我说了算,就是煮着吃!"

"这事儿该听我的,非烤不行!"

两人争执不下,一直吵到村里的长辈面前。老人家给他们出了个主意:射下来的大雁,一半煮着吃,一半烤着吃。哥儿俩都同意了。

随后他们再去射雁,发现那群大雁早已飞得无影无踪了。

【寓意】做任何事情都应该当机立断,说干就干。无休止的讨论,滔滔不绝的空谈,对于事业只有百害而无一利。事情要分清本末主次和轻重缓急。我们不能本末倒置,否则将一事无成。

寓言故事

Brothers Arguing over Wild Geese

From *Ying Xie Lu*

Once two brothers went out hunting and saw a flock of the wild geese flying in the distance, so they set up their bows and arrows and got ready to shoot them.

The elder brother said, "Since the wild geese are fat, we should **stew** them after shooting them down."

The younger brother objected, "It's better to stew the big geese for eating, but the wild geese should be roasted, **fragrant** and crispy."

"I'm in charge, and it's stewed and eaten!"

"You should listen to me on this matter, and they have to be roasted!"

They argued with each other all the way to the elder in the village. The elder gave them an idea: after shooting down a wild goose, they can stew a half of it and roast another half. They both agreed.

Then they went back to shoot the wild geese, and found that the flock of wild geese had already flown away without a trace.

❋ **Moral**

To achieve our goals we should make a decisive decision instantly and just do it right away. For our cause,

stew

v. 煮

fragrant

adj. 香的

the endless discussion and empty quarrel bring lots of harm and no benefit at all. It is necessary for us to distinguish significances as well as **priorities**. We can't put the cart before the horse, otherwise nothing will be achieved.

priority
n. 优先事项, 首要事情

宣王好射

《尹文子》

  齐宣王爱好射箭,还特别喜欢听人夸他能拉硬弓。实际上他使的弓,只用三石(约180斤)的力气就能拉开。左右随从摸透了他的脾气,专挑好听的字眼儿说,什么"后羿再世"啦,什么"铁臂神弓"啦,把齐宣王捧得晕晕乎乎,连东南西北也分不清了。

  他把这张弓交给左右的人传看。身边的人都试着拉,但只把弓拉到一半,就装着拉不动的样子,恭维地说:"这张弓没有九石(约540斤)的力气拉不开。除了大王,谁还能够使用这张弓呢?"齐宣王听了非常高兴。

  其实,齐宣王用的不过是三石力的弓,可是他始终以为自己拉的是九石力的弓。

【寓意】一个人如果只喜欢听奉承的话,就不能够正确地认识自己。

King Xuan Loving Archery

From *Yinwenzi*

The King Xuan of Qi State loved archery and especially liked to be **bragged** about his ability to draw a hard bow. In fact, his bow could be drawn with the strength of only three *dan* (about 90 kilograms). His attendants, who understood his temper, picked out some nice words to say, such as "reincarnation of Hou Yi (Crack Archer in ancient Chinese legends)" or "iron arms and magical bow", which made the King Xuan of Qi so dizzy that he couldn't even distinguish the four directions, east, south, west and north.

He handed the bow to those people around him, so as to pass it on. Those around him all tried to pull it, but stopped halfway, flattering, "The bow cannot be drawn without the strength of nine *dan* (about 270 kilograms). Who else can use the bow except for the King?" The King was very happy to hear.

In fact, the King Xuan of Qi was using a bow with only three-*dan* power, but he always thought that he was drawing a bow with nine-*dan* power.

brag
v. 吹嘘

Moral

If a person only likes to be flattered, he will not be able to know himself properly.

薛谭学讴

《列子》

　　战国时期有个人叫薛谭,他向秦国歌唱家秦青学习声乐。一段时间后,薛谭觉得已经学得八九不离十,没什么好学的了,于是向老师请辞回家。秦青没有阻止他,还在郊外大路旁设宴为他送行。

　　当时,正值春暖花开季节,早春的城外风景让师生俩陶醉在生机勃勃的春风里。秦青情不自禁地打着节拍,高歌一曲。歌声里充满对生活的热爱和对师生惜别的深情,那歌声在林间低回,在云间缭绕。薛谭从未听过这样曼妙的歌声,突然感到自己和老师的巨大差距,知道自己错了,心生悔意,马上向老师道歉,请老师原谅他,给他重新回到老师身边继续学习的机会。

　　从此以后,薛谭毕生追随老师秦青,把老师的歌唱艺术发扬光大。

【寓意】学习是永无止境的,不能小有成绩就骄傲自满,要虚心好学,持之以恒。

 寓言故事

Xue Tan Learning to Sing

From *Liezi*

During the Warring States Period, there was a man named Xue Tan, who learned vocal music from Qin Qing, a famous singer of Qi State. After a period of time, Xue Tan felt that he had learned almost everything and had nothing more to learn, so he asked his teacher for **resignation** and going back home. Qin Qing did not stop him and held a banquet to see him off by the roadside in the suburbs.

It was the season, warm and **abloom**, and the scenery outside the city in the early spring made both the student and the teacher indulge in the vibrant spring breeze. Qin Qing couldn't help beating the time and singing a song. The song was full of love for life and affectionate farewells to each other, which echoed in the forest and lingered among the clouds. Xue Tan, who had never heard such a graceful song before, suddenly felt the huge gap between himself and his teacher, and knew that he was wrong and regretful. He apologized to his teacher immediately, asking his teacher to forgive him and give him a chance to go back to his teacher and continue his study.

From then on, Xue Tan followed his teacher Qin Qing all his life and carried forward the singing art of his teacher.

resignation

n. 请辞

abloom

adj. 开花的

Moral

The story goes that learning is never-ending. Thus, we should not be complacent with small achievements, but be open-minded and **industrious** with perseverance.

industrious
adj. 勤劳的

掩耳盗铃

《吕氏春秋》

春秋时候，晋国大夫范氏由于争权夺利失败，被世家赵氏所灭。他携家人仓皇出逃，家产被百姓和仇敌抢劫一空。

一天，一个小偷摸进范家院子里，发现院子里吊着一口大钟，钟是用上等青铜铸成的，造型和图案都很精美。小偷乐坏了，心想：把它卖掉，一定能赚不少钱。

小偷试着去背走那口钟，但太重了，背不动。他想把钟砸碎了，分批拿回去，但砸钟的声音会惊动所有人，他不敢。怎么办呢？他突然想起一个妙招，之所以会听到声音，是因为耳朵的缘故。如果把耳朵堵起来，不就听不见声音了吗？于是，他找来棉絮，把自己的耳朵堵得死死的，一点声音也听不见，然后就放心大胆地砸起钟来。

一下一下，响亮的钟声传到很远的地方。人们听到钟声蜂拥而至，把小偷捉住了。

【寓意】闭目塞听是自欺欺人的做法，结果遭人嘲笑。

Covering One's Ears to Steal a Bell

From *Master Lü's Spring and Autumn Annals*

During the Spring and Autumn Period, the head of Fan clan, senior official of Jin State, was defeated in a struggle scrambling for power and profit by its rival the Zhao clan. He and his family **deserted** their homestead and fled elsewhere. All their property was looted out by his enemies and local residents.

desert
v. 舍弃，逃走

One day, a thief wanted to steal something from Fan's house and saw a big bell hung over the courtyard, which was made of the best bronze with the exquisite shape and pattern. The thief was so happy to think that he could make a lot of money by stealing and selling it.

The thief tried to carry away the bell, but it was too heavy to move. He wanted to **smash** the bell into pieces and take its pieces back in batches. However, smashing the bell would sound an alarm on everyone, so he didn't dare. What to do? He suddenly came up with a brilliant trick: the reason why he could hear sound was that his ears were working. If he **plugged up** his ears, he wouldn't be able to hear the sound, right? Then, he found some cotton fibre to plug his ears so that he could not hear a sound at all, and assuredly struck the bell.

smash
v. 打碎

plug up
把……塞住

One by one, the bell sounded loudly and spread far

away. When people heard the bell, they swarmed to catch the thief.

❖ Moral

To close one's eyes and plug one's ears only fool oneself, which results in **ridicule**.

ridicule

n. 嘲笑，讥笑

燕人还国

《吕氏春秋》

　　从前，有一个人在燕国出生，在楚国长大，直至花甲之年还不曾回过家乡。由于思乡心切，他不顾年事已高，气血衰退，居然独自一人不辞劳苦，千里迢迢去寻故里。

　　在半路上，他遇到一个北上的人。两人自我介绍后，很快结伴而行。到了晋国的地界时，同伴和这个燕国人开了一个大玩笑。他指着前面的晋国城郭说道："你马上就要到家了，前面就是燕国的城镇。"燕人一听，一股浓厚的乡情骤然涌上心头，一时激动得说不出话来，两眼被泪水模糊了，脸上怆然失色。过了一会儿，那同伴指着路边的土神庙说："这就是你家乡的土神庙。"燕人听了，马上叹息起来。家乡的土神庙是曾保佑自己先辈在这块燕国的土地上繁衍生息的圣地啊！他们继续往前走，同伴又指着路边的一栋房屋说："那就是你的先辈住过的房屋。"燕人听了这话，顿时热泪盈眶，滚滚的泪水把他的衣衫也弄湿了。祖居不仅是父母、祖辈生活过的地方，而且是自己初生的摇篮，那里有多少动人的往事和令人怀念的、神圣而珍贵的东西啊！那同伴看到自己的谎话让燕人坚信不疑，自鸣得意，又想捉弄他，指着附近的一座土堆说："那就是你家的祖坟。"燕人一听，更是悲从中来，马上跪倒在祖坟前，磕头不止。这个燕人虽然已年至花甲，但是他站在阔别多年的先辈坟前，感到自己像一个失去了爹娘的孤苦伶仃的孩子，再也禁不住强烈的心酸，一个劲地放声痛哭起来。同伴看到燕人悲痛不止的样子，哈哈大笑起来，对燕人说："算了，算了，别把身子哭坏了。我刚才是骗你的。这里只是晋国，离燕国还有几百里地。"

　　听了同伴这么一说，燕人知道上当了。他怀乡念旧的虔诚心情顿时烟消云散，对自己轻信别人而导致的行为感到难堪。等到了燕国，真的见到燕

寓言故事

国的城楼和土地庙,真的见到先人的房舍和坟墓,悲凄心情反而淡薄了。

【寓意】燕人对家乡故土的思念之情是真实感人的,同伴的恶作剧亵渎了燕人的感情,也破坏了燕人的心情,让他感到上当受辱。即使是最好的朋友,也要有交往的距离,不是什么玩笑都可以开的。掌握分寸既是尊重他人,也是修行自己。

用英语讲中国好故事

A Man of Yan Returning to His Hometown

From *Master Lü's Spring and Autumn Annals*

Once upon a time, a man, born in Yan State, grew up in Chu State but he never returned to his hometown until he was in his sixties. Since he was rather homesick, he went all the way to his hometown alone, despite his old age and his declining **vitality**.

Halfway there, he met a man going to the north. The two introduced themselves and soon traveled in companionship. When they reached the border of Jin State, the companion played a big joke on the man of Yan. He pointed to the city of Jin in front of him and said, "You will soon be home, and ahead is the town of Yan." When the man of Yan heard this, a strong feeling of homeliness suddenly came over him, and he was so excited that he could not speak, his eyes blurred by tears, and his face **pathos-stricken**. After a while, the companion pointed to the temple of local Land-God by the roadside and said, "This is the temple of Land-God in your hometown." When the man of Yan heard this, he immediately sighed. It was a holy place in his hometown that had blessed his ancestors to flourish in this land of Yan! As they went on, the companion pointed to a house by the roadside and said,

---

vitality

n. 活力,生命力

pathos-stricken

adj. 感伤的

寓言故事

"That is the house where your ancestors lived." When the man of Yan heard that, he **burst into tears**, and the rolling tears wetted his shirt. The ancestral house was not only the place where his parents and ancestors had lived, but also the cradle of his own **infancy**, and how many touching past events and nostalgic, sacred and precious things were there! The companion, seeing that he had convinced the man of his lies, feeling smug, and wanting to play a trick on him, pointed to a nearby mound and said, "That is your ancestral grave." Upon hearing this, the man was even more saddened, and immediately fell on his knees before the ancestral grave, kowtowing. Although the man of Yan was already in his sixties, he stood in front of the graves of his ancestors who had been separated for many years, and he felt like a lonely and helpless child who had lost his parents. When the companion saw the grief from the man of Yan, he laughed and said to the man, "Never mind, never mind, don't cry to harm your body. I was lying to you just now. This is only the kingdom of Jin, still several hundred miles away from Yan State."

Hearing this from his companion, the man of Yan knew he had been **deceived**. His nostalgic devotion to his homeland evaporated, and he was embarrassed by his own **gullibility** in believing others. However, when the man really arrived in his homeland and saw the buildings and temples of Yan, as well as the houses and graves of his ancestors, his sadness faded instead.

burst into tears
突然哭起来

infancy
n. 婴儿期，幼儿期

deceive
v. 欺骗

gullibility
n. 容易受骗

165

Moral

The man of Yan really cherishes the memory of his native land, but the pranks from his companion **desecrate** his innocence and spoil his mood, making him feel cheated and humiliated. Even best friends need to interact properly rather than play any jokes at will. It is both respect for others and also perfection of oneself for one to do.

desecrate
v. 亵渎

叶公好龙

《新序》

　　从前,有位叶公,特别喜欢龙。他屋内的梁、柱、门、窗上,都请巧匠刻上龙的图案,雪白的墙上,也请工匠画上一条条巨龙,甚至他穿的衣服、盖的被子、挂的蚊帐上,也都绣上了活灵活现的金龙。

　　方圆几百里的人,都知道叶公好龙。天上的真龙听说以后,很受感动,亲自下来探望叶公。巨龙把身子盘在叶公家客堂的柱子上,尾巴拖在方砖地上,头从窗户里伸进了叶公的书房。

　　叶公一见真龙,顿时吓得面色苍白,转身逃跑了。

【寓意】叶公口头上说的和实际上的行为截然相反,虚假的爱经不起实际检验。像叶公这样口是心非的人,是个伪君子。

Lord Ye's Love for Dragons

From *Anecdotes Compiled by Liu Xiang*

Once upon a time, there was a much respected man called Lord Ye, who **was** particularly **fond of** dragons. The beams, pillars, doors and windows of his house were all engraved with dragon motifs by skilled craftsmen, the snow-white walls were painted with giant dragons, and even his clothes, quilts and mosquito nets he hung were embroidered with vivid golden dragons.

Everyone within a radius of several hundred miles knew that Lord Ye was particularly fond of dragons. When a dragon in heaven heard, he was so moved that he came down to visit Lord Ye himself. The giant dragon coiled his body on the pillars of Lord Ye's guest hall, its tail dragging on the square-brick floor, and its head sticking through the window into Lord Ye's study.

At the sight of the real dragon, Lord Ye was so frightened that he turned round and fled.

Moral

Lord Ye's verbal words are diametrically opposed to his actual actions, which proves that false love cannot withstand actual tests. A man like Lord Ye who affirms with his lips but denies in his heart is a **hypocrite**.

be fond of
喜爱

hypocrite
n. 伪君子

寓言故事

疑邻偷斧

《吕氏春秋》

从前,有一个人丢了一把斧头。他怀疑是隔壁的小孩偷的,于是就暗中观察小孩的行动,果然看他很像偷了斧子的样子。他看那个孩子走路的姿势,像是偷了斧子的样子;他观察那个孩子的神色,也像是偷了斧子的样子;他听那个孩子说话的语气,更像是偷了斧子的样子。总之,在他的眼里,那个孩子的一举一动,都像是偷斧子的样子。后来,他就断定邻居的儿子偷了他的斧子。

隔了几天,他在后山找到了遗失的斧头,原来是自己上山砍柴时弄丢了。

第二天,他又遇到了邻居的儿子。此时,他再去观察邻居家的小孩,一举一动丝毫也不像偷过斧子的样子了。

【寓意】个人的主观成见会影响其对客观事物真相的判断。对人对事,都不要先入为主,要经过调查研究再做出判断,绝对不能毫无根据地瞎猜疑,否则往往会产生错觉。

Suspecting the Neighbor of Stealing an Axe

From *Master Lü's Spring and Autumn Annals*

Once upon a time, there was a man who lost an axe. He suspected that his neighbor's son had stolen it. So he decided to closely observe the neighbor's son. As a result, the neighbor's son began to appear like a thief who had stolen an axe. His neighbor's son walked liked an axe thief, looked like an axe thief, and even talked like an axe thief. To sum up, in the man's eyes, the child's each and every move seemed that he had stolen the axe. In the end, the man concluded that it was the neighbor's son who had stolen his axe.

After a few days, the axe was found in the back of the hill and it turned out that he had left it there when he went up the hill to cut firewood.

The following day, he met the neighbor's son again. This time, the man found that the child did not look one little bit like an axe thief.

Moral

One's subjective **preconceptions** will affect one's judgment of objective truth. It is important not to have preconceived ideas about anyone or anything in advance,

preconception
n. 成见，预想

寓言故事

but to make a judgment after investigation and research. We shall never make blind suspicions without any basis, or **misconceptions** will often arise.

misconception
n. 误解

永某氏之鼠

《柳河东集》

古时候，永州有一个十分迷信的人。他属鼠，就把老鼠奉为神物，不让家里人养猫逮鼠，听凭老鼠在粮仓、厨房横行。

于是，周围的老鼠都搬到他这里来安家。大白天，老鼠成群结队地在屋子里乱窜，肆无忌惮地在主人脚下追逐；夜晚，老鼠争食打架，吱吱怪叫，吵得他们无法入睡。他家的家具都被老鼠啃得千疮百孔，箱柜里的衣物也被咬成布屑碎片，就连全家人的一日三餐，也都是老鼠吃剩下的。但是，这个主人听之任之，严禁家人捕捉老鼠。

几年以后，这家人搬到别的地方去住了。新来的主人看见老鼠猖獗的情景，惊呆了："老鼠是最可恶的东西，怎么能听凭它们猖狂到这等地步！"新主人借来了五六只善于捕鼠的大猫，又雇了几个帮工，把所有的门户全都封死，把屋顶的砖瓦全部揭开，看见鼠洞，先是烟熏，再是水灌，最后逐个堵死。结果，被捕杀的老鼠堆成了小山，被运到偏僻的地方，那腐烂的臭味过了几个月才散尽。

【寓意】小人得志虽然能嚣张一时，但是不能长久。因此，依仗权势的小人会遭到彻底被消灭的下场。

Nobody's Rats in Yongzhou

From *Anthology of Liu Hedong*

In ancient times, there was a very **superstitious** person in Yongzhou Prefecture. Born in the Year of the Rat, he worshipped rats as a king of sacred animals, so he did not let his family keep cats to catch rats, but allowed rats to run amok in his family's granary and kitchen.

As a result, all the rats in the neighborhood moved to his house to settle down. In the daylight, the rats **scampered** around the house in groups, chasing at their masters' feet with impunity; at night, rats fought for food and squeaked so loudly that they could not sleep. The furniture of his house was gnawed with lots of holes by the rats, the clothes in the chests and cabinets were also bitten into scraps of cloth, and even the three meals for the whole family every day were all leftover by the rats. However, the owner let the rats do as they pleased and forbade his family to catch them.

A few years later, the family moved to another place to live. The new owner was shocked to see the **rampant** rats, "Rats are the most **abominable** things. How can they be allowed to go so wild?" The new owner borrowed five or six big cats that were good at catching rats, and hired several helpers, sealing all the doors and gates,

superstitous
adj. 迷信的

scamper
v. 蹦蹦跳跳

rampant
adj. 泛滥的
abominable
adj. 令人憎恶的

and uncovering all the bricks and tiles on the roof. On seeing the rat holes, they firstly used smoke, then water, and finally blocked the holes one by one. As a result, the rats being caught and killed were piled up into a small mountain and transported to remote places. There, the stench of decaying rats took several months to **dissipate**.

dissipate
v. 消散，消失

❖ Moral

Owing to his success, a villain can be **arrogant** for a while, but not forever. Furthermore, the one who relies on power and influence will be completely wiped out.

arrogant
adj. 自大的

鹬蚌相争

《战国策》

战国时候，秦国最强，经常侵略弱国。弱国之间，也经常互有摩擦。有一次，赵国声称要攻打燕国。苏代受燕王的委托，到赵国去劝阻赵王。

赵惠文王知道苏代的来意，明知故问："苏代，你来见我，有什么事吗？"苏代回答："尊敬的大王，我给您讲故事来了。"苏代讲了下面这个故事：

蚌趁着天晴，张开两片硬壳，在河滩上晒太阳。有只鹬鸟见了，快速地把嘴伸进蚌壳里去啄肉。蚌急忙把硬壳合上，钳住鹬鸟的嘴不放。鹬鸟啄肉不成，嘴反被钳住，便威胁蚌说："好吧，你不松开壳就等着。今天不下雨，明天不下雨，把你干死！"蚌毫不示弱地回敬："好吧，你的嘴已被我钳住。今天拔不出，明天拔不出，把你饿死！"

就这样，蚌和鹬鸟在河滩上互相争持，谁也不让谁。时间一长，它们都精疲力竭。正好有个渔翁经过这里，见它们死死缠在一起，谁也不能动弹，便轻易地把它们一起捉住，拿回了家。

苏代讲完故事，对赵惠文王说："如果赵国去攻伐燕国，燕国竭力抵抗，双方必然长久相持不下，弄得疲惫不堪。这样，强大的秦国就会像渔翁那样坐收其利。请大王认真考虑再作决定吧。"

赵惠王觉得苏代说的有道理，就打消了攻打燕国的念头。

【寓意】"鹬蚌相争，渔翁得利"比喻如果双方相持不下，结果会两败俱伤，使他人得利。

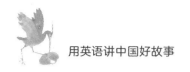

A Snipe and a Clam Locked in Fight

From *Stratagems of the Warring States*

During the Warring States Period, Qin State was the strongest power and often invaded other weak states. The weak ones often fought against each other. Once, Zhao State claimed to attack Yan State, and Su Dai was commissioned by the King of Yan to go to Zhao State, so as to dissuade the King of Zhao from attacking Yan State.

King Huiwen of Zhao got the intention of Su Dai and knowingly asked, "Su Dai, what is your business in coming to see me?" Su replied, "Your Majesty, I have come to tell you a story." Su Dai told the following story:

One day, a clam opened its shells to **bask** in the sun on a bench. Suddenly, a snipe quickly stuck its beak into the clam. The latter hastily closed its shells and clamped down on the snipe's beak, and did not let it go. The snipe could not peck at meat but its beak was clamped, so it threatened the clam, saying, "All right, if you don't let go of your shells, you will have to wait. If it doesn't rain today, nor tomorrow, you will die of thirst!" The clam responded back with no sign of weakness, "Well, your mouth has been clamped by me. If you can't pull it out today, nor tomorrow, you'll starve to death!"

The clam and the snipe fought each other on the bench,

bask

v. 晒太阳

neither being willing to let the other win. As time passed, they were both exhausted. Finally, a fisherman came along and saw them **entangled** deadly, so he easily caught them together and took them home.

After Su Dai finished telling the story, he said to King Huiwen of Zhao, "If Zhao attacks Yan and Yan **resists** with all its might, the two sides are bound to be at loggerheads for a long time and will certainly be exhausted for a long time. Then, the powerful Qin State will be like the fisherman who reaps the benefits of the fight. Your Majesty, please seriously consider it before making a decision."

The King of Zhao felt that Su Dai's words were reasonable, so he gave up the idea of attacking Yan.

entangled
adj. 纠缠的

resist
v. 抵抗

❖ Moral

The metaphor is that when two sides are at loggerheads, that will lead to a lose-lose situation, making others gain profits.

177

凿井得人

《吕氏春秋》

宋国有个姓丁的,家里没有井。做饭、浇菜地,都要用水。他家只得派一个劳动力,每天到村外去挑水。

后来,姓丁的在家里打了一口井,用水就很方便了。姓丁的逢人便说:"我家凿了一口井,等于得了一个人。"

这话三传两传便走了样,说成:"丁家凿井挖出一个活人来了。"越传越奇,越奇越传,最后传到宋国国君的耳朵里。

宋君就派人到丁家调查。姓丁的说:"我说的是凿了一口井等于得了一个劳动力,不是说从井里挖出一个活人来呀。"

【寓意】我们要懂得辨别信息的真伪,不要对所有的事情一概听而信之,也不要在自己证实前就进行传播,以免以讹传讹。

寓言故事

The Man Who Was Found in Well

From *Master Lü's Spring and Autumn Annals*

In Song State, there was a man with the surname of Ding, whose family had no well. Water is needed for cooking and watering vegetables. His family had to send a man to go outside the village to fetch water every day.

Later, Ding's family dug a well by their house, which made it very convenient to fetch water. The man surnamed Ding said at every meeting, "My family dug a well, equal to a laborer."

The statement **went astray** after being spread a few times, "Ding's family dug a well and dug out a living man." The more it spread, the stranger it became, and vice versa. It reached the King's ears finally.

go astray
迷路，偏离正轨

The ruler then sent someone to Ding's family to investigate. Ding said, "What I said is not digging out a living man from a well but digging a well equal to a living laborer."

❀ Moral

We should learn to discern the false from the genuine. Don't believe everything you hear and do not repost or **retweet** them before verification, so that they will not be wrongly informed.

retweet
v. 转发

曾子杀猪

《韩非子》

一天早晨,曾子的夫人要去赶集,儿子哭闹着也要一起去。

集市又远又乱,带孩子去不方便。曾子的夫人就哄孩子说:"你在家等我,你不是爱吃猪肉吗?我回家就杀猪烧肉给你吃。"孩子听妈妈说有猪肉吃,就乖乖回家了。

快到中午时,曾子的夫人从集市回来了,就见曾子抓住一头猪要杀。孩子妈妈连忙制止他说:"刚才是哄他回家,随便说的。"

曾子说:"这可不能开玩笑啊!小孩子不懂事,最相信大人的话,父母就是他的学习榜样,如今你哄骗他,是教他学会骗人。母亲骗儿子,做儿子的就不会相信自己的母亲,以后也不会相信其他人,这不是正确教育孩子的方法。"

于是,夫妻俩杀了猪,兑现了诺言。

【寓意】曾子用自己的行动教育孩子要言而有信,诚实无诈。同时这个故事也教育成人,自己的言行对孩子影响很大,身教重于言教。

Why Zengzi Killed the Pig

From *Hanfeizi*

One morning, the wife of Zengzi was going to the market, and her son was crying for going together with her.

The market was far away and **chaotic**, so it was not convenient for Zengzi's wife to go with her child. Thus, the wife **coaxed** her son, "Wait for me at home. Don't you love pork? After I go home and I'll kill a pig and cook pork for you." The child heard it and stayed at home.

It was almost at noon when the wife came back from the market and saw her husband Zengzi catching hold of a pig to kill. She stopped him hastily and said, "I said that for coaxing him back home."

Zengzi said, "It is no joke! The child is not sensible, but he believes most in the words of adults. Thus, his parents are his role models, but you are teaching him to lie if you coax him. When the mother lies to her son, the son will not trust his own mother, nor will he trust anyone else in the future. It is not a right way to educate a child."

Thus, the couple killed the pig and fulfilled their promise.

chaotic
adj. 混乱的
coax
v. 哄骗

Moral

By taking actions Zengzi taught his child to be true to his words and be honest in his actions. The story also teaches adults that their own words and actions have great influences on their children, and that it is better to teach children by examples than by words.

寓言故事

折箭训子

《魏书》

南朝时候,少数民族吐谷浑(Tǔyùhún)的首领阿豺有二十个儿子。

有一天,阿豺对他们说:"你们每人给我拿一支箭来。"

儿子们每人奉上一支箭。阿豺当着他们的面把二十支箭一一折断,扔到地下,然后又让儿子们每人拿一支箭给叔叔慕利延。他叫慕利延先拿一支箭把它折断,慕利延拿起一支箭毫不费力地折为两截。

阿豺又说:"你把剩下来的十九支箭握成一把,一起折断。"

慕利延用尽全身的力气都没能折断。

阿豺指着这一把箭对儿子们说:"你们明白了吗?一支箭是容易被折断的,一把箭就很难被折断。只有大家齐心协力,我们的国家才能富强!"

【寓意】一箭易折,十箭难断。团结就是力量。个人的力量是有限的,众人拾柴火焰高,人心齐泰山移。

Breaking Arrows to Admonish Sons

From *Historical Book of Northern Wei Dynasty*

During the Southern Dynasty, A-Chai, a leader of the ethnic minority Tuyuhun, had twenty sons.

One day, A-Chai said to his sons, "Each of you bring me an arrow."

After each of his sons brought an arrow, A-Chai broke each of the twenty arrows in front of his sons and threw them on the ground. Then he asked each of his sons to bring one more arrow to his uncle Muli Yan. He told Muli Yan to take one of the arrows and break it, and Muli Yan took it and broke it into two parts without difficulty.

A-Chai said, "You hold the remaining nineteen arrows together and break them."

With all his strength, Muli Yan was unable to break it.

A-Chai pointed to the handful of arrows and said to his sons, "Do you understand? An arrow is easy to break; a handful of arrows are difficult to break. Only when we all unite to work together can our country be rich and strong!"

Moral

One arrow is easy to break; ten arrows are difficult to break. The strength of an individual is limited, but unity is strength. The flame can rise as everyone gathers wood and Mount Tai can be moved as people's hearts are united.

寓言故事

郑人逃暑

《苻子》

　　有个郑国人怕热,就到一棵大树下乘凉。

　　太阳在移动,大树的影子也随之变化,他也跟着树荫不断地挪动凉席,免得晒太阳。到了晚上,月亮从东边升起来,慢慢地向西边移动,大树的影子也随之缓缓移动。郑人还像白天一样,又随着树影挪动自己的凉席,结果,他的衣服全被露水打湿了。

　　这个人白天乘凉的办法很巧妙,但晚上用同样办法乘凉就相当笨拙了。

【寓意】事物都处在不断变化之中,要因时而变,与时俱进。如果我们教条地照搬过去的做法,往往会碰壁,贻笑大方。

A Man of Zheng Escaping Summer Heat

From *Fuzi*

A man of Zheng State couldn't stand heat, so he went under a big tree to enjoy the cool.

As the sun moved, the shadow of the tree changed, and he also kept moving his cool mat with the shade to avoid sunshine. At night, the moon rose from the east and slowly went towards the west, and the shade of the tree moved slowly with it. The man also moved his cool mat with the shade of the tree as he did during the day. As a result, his clothes were all wet with **dew**.

The man's method of enjoying the cool during the day is very clever, but it is quite clumsy to enjoy the cool in the same way at night.

dew

n. 露，露水

❖ Moral

Things are constantly changing with the times, so we should also change. Instead, if we dogmatically copy the past practice, we will often run into trouble and expose ourselves to ridicule.

郑人惜鱼

《宋文宪公全集》

从前,郑国有一个人自称非常爱鱼。在他家的庭院里,摆放着三只大鱼缸,养了好多种鱼。这些鱼,有的是他用网捕到的,有的是他从湖里钓的,有的是从集市上买的,有的是从朋友那里讨来的。

他认为,鱼儿离不开水,把鱼儿养起来,就是他爱鱼的最好方式。他没有想过,不论以什么方式得到鱼,鱼被人抓的过程中,因为脱水都很疲惫,即使放入鱼缸重新回到水里,刚开始的时候,大都翻起白色的肚皮,浮在水面,吃力地喘气。

郑人看到那些鱼无精打采,就捧出来看着说:"鳞没有受伤吧?是不是生病了?"实在看不出有受伤的地方,就以为是鱼饿了,他拿来谷末和麦麸,撒到鱼缸里,搞得鱼缸里的水都浑浊了。

有人对他说:"鱼儿本来生活在江河里,你把他们养在这样小的鱼缸里,每天还要抓在手上玩弄它,嘴上说'我爱鱼,我爱鱼',其实你是在害鱼啊!"

郑国人根本听不进去。没过三天,水缸里的鱼全因为鳞片脱落而死,郑国人这时才后悔没有听别人的话。

【寓意】郑人违背自然规律,按照自己的主观意志办事,结果好心做了错事。

A Man of Zheng Who Cherished Fish

From *Complete Works by Song Lian*

Once upon a time, a man of Zheng State claimed to love fish very much. In his courtyard, there were three large fish tanks in which he bred many fishes. Some of them were caught with nets, some fished from lakes, some bought from markets, and others asked for from his friends.

He believed that fish could not live without water, and that breeding those fish was the best way to show his love for them. He didn't think about the fact that no matter how the fish were obtained, during the process of being caught they were exhausted without water. Even when they were put into the tanks and returned to the water, at first most of them turned up their white bellies, floated on the surface, and strained to breathe.

When the man saw those fish **languishing**, he held them outside the water and said, "Is there nothing wrong with the fish's scales? Are they sick?" The man couldn't really see any injuries, so he thought the fish were hungry. He brought in grain dregs and wheat bran and sprinkled them into the fish tanks, making water of the tanks **turbid**.

Someone told him, "The fish would have lived in the river, but you kept them in such small fish tanks and

languish

v. 受煎熬

turbid

adj. 浑浊的

grabbed them in your hands for enjoying. You said, 'I love the fish, I love the fish,' but actually you are harming the fish!"

The man of Zheng didn't listen to those words at all. In the following three days, all the fish in the tanks died because their scales fell off. It was only then that the man regretted not listening to others' words.

❖ Moral

The man of Zheng went against the laws of nature, did things according to his own will, and **spoiled** things with his good intentions.

spoil

v. 破坏，损坏

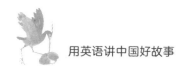
用英语讲中国好故事

捉蝉的学问

《庄子》

有一天,天气很热,孔子带着学生们来到楚国。他们走进一片密林中歇凉,林中蝉声一片。有一位驼背老人手拿一根顶端涂有树脂的竹竿在捉蝉,只见他一粘一只,百发百中。大家在一旁看得入了迷。

孔子问老汉:"您捉蝉的本领可真大!这里边有什么奥妙吗?"老汉笑笑说:"如果一定要说奥妙,当然也是有的。蝉是很机灵的,一有动静,它就飞了。因此,先要练得手拿竹竿纹丝不动。练到竹竿顶端能放两粒弹丸而不掉下来,捉蝉就有一定的把握了;练到放三粒弹丸而不掉下来,捉十只蝉顶多逃脱一只;练到放五粒弹丸而不掉下来,捉蝉就像伸手拣东西一样容易了。手不抖,身躯也不能动。我站着的时候,像纹丝不动的树干;手拿竹竿的胳膊,像树上伸出去的老枝,不颤不摇。捉蝉的时候,我专心致志,天地万物都不能扰乱我的注意力,眼睛里看到的只是蝉的翅膀。能够练到这样的地步,您还怕捉不到蝉吗?"

孔子听了,教育学生说:"听明白了没有?只有锲而不舍、专心致志,才能把本领练到出神入化的地步啊!"

【寓意】成功没有捷径可走。要做成一件事,需要善于观察、专心致志、勤学苦练、讲究方法,才能练就过硬本领。

寓言故事

Know How to Catch Cicadas

From *Zhuangzi*

On a hot day, Confucius took his students to Chu State. They went into a dense forest to cool off, where the sound of cicadas was heard. A **hunchbacked** old man, holding a bamboo pole with a resin-coated tip, was catching cicadas without any missing. Everyone watched in fascination.

Confucius asked the old man, "You are really great at catching cicadas! Are there any secrets in it?" The old man laughed and said, "If I must say there is a secret, of course there is. The cicadas are very clever, and they will fly away at the first sign of movement and noise. Therefore, the first thing you need to do is to practice holding the bamboo pole still. If you can hold the pole until you can put two **projectiles** on its top without falling, you will be able to catch cicadas with certainty; if putting three projectiles without falling, at most one out of ten cicadas can escape; if five projectiles without falling, catching the cicada will be as easy as reaching for something with your hand. I don't shake my hands and move my body. When I stand, I am like an immobile tree trunk; when I hold a bamboo pole in my hands, my arms are like the old branches sticking out of a tree, not trembling or shaking. When I

hunchback

n. 驼背

projectile

n. 弹丸

was catching cicadas, I was so focused that nothing in the world could distract my attention, and all I could see were the cicadas' wings. If you can practice to such an extent, are you still afraid that you won't be able to catch the cicadas?"

After hearing those words, Confucius taught his students, "Do you understand? Only with perseverance and dedication can you practice your skills to the point of mastery."

Moral

There are no **shortcuts** to success. In order to achieve something, we need to be observant, attentive, diligent and methodical, so as to develop excellent skills.

shortcut

n. 捷径